D1606831

IN THE PROMISED LAND

THE BIBLE
AND
ITS STORY

1
THE CREATION

2
THE PATRIARCHS
AND MOSES

3
IN THE PROMISED LAND

4
KINGS AND PROPHETS

5
EXILE AND RETURN

6
JESUS THE CHRIST

7
THE LORD'S FOLLOWERS

Planned and produced by
Jaca Book — Le Centurion
from the ideas of
Charles Ehlinger, Hervé Lauriot Prévost,
Pierre Talec, and the editorial committee
of Jaca Book

A chapter outline for this volume
is printed on the last two pages
of the volume.

IN THE PROMISED LAND

THE BIBLE AND ITS STORY

Text by Pierre Talec
Translation by Kenneth D. Whitehead
Illustrations by Vittorio Belli, Sandro Corsi,
Antonio Molino, Sergio Molino, Franco Vignazia

 Winston Press 430 Oak Grove Minneapolis, Minnesota 55403

Published in Italy under the title
Nella Terra Promessa
Copyright © 1982 Jaca Book – Le Centurion

**Licensed publisher and distributor
of the English-language edition:**
Winston Press, Inc.
430 Oak Grove
Minneapolis, MN 55403
United States of America

Agents:
Canada –
LeDroit/Novalis-Select
135 Nelson Street
Ottawa, Ontario
Canada K1N 7R4

Australia, New Zealand, New Guinea, Fiji Islands –
Dove Communications, Pty. Ltd.
Suite 1 60-64 Railway Road
Blackburn, Victoria 3130
Australia

Acknowledgements:
All Scripture quotations, unless otherwise
indicated, are taken from the *Revised
Standard Version Common Bible,* copyright ©
1973 by the Division of Christian Education
of the National Council of the Churches of
Christ in the U.S.A. Used by permission.

All Scripture quotations indicated by *TEV*
(Today's English Version) are from the
Good News Bible – Old Testament: Copyright ©
American Bible Society 1976; New Testament:
Copyright © American Bible Society, 1966,
1971, 1976.

Winston Scriptural Consultant:
Catherine Litecky, CSJ
Department of Theology
College of St. Catherine

Winston Staff:
Lois Welshons, Hermann Weinlick – editorial
Reg Sandland, Kathe Wilcoxon – design

Jaca Book – Le Centurion Editorial Committee:
Maretta Campi, Charles Ehlinger,
Enrico Galbiati, Elio Guerriero, Pierre Talec

Color selection: Carlo Scotti, Milan
Printing: Gorenjski tisk, Kranj, Yugoslavia

Copyright © 1983, English-language edition,
Jaca Book – Le Centurion. All rights reserved.
Printed in Yugoslavia.

Library of Congress Catalog Card Number: 82-51201
ISBN: 0-86683-193-2

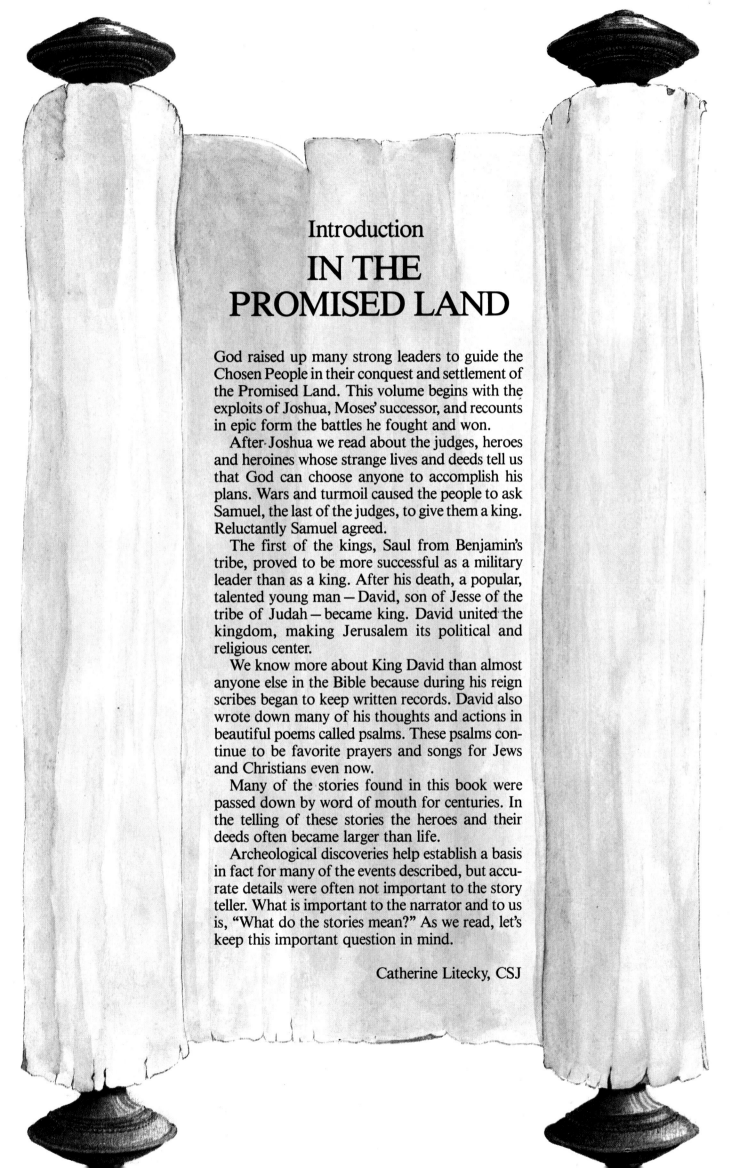

Introduction
IN THE
PROMISED LAND

God raised up many strong leaders to guide the Chosen People in their conquest and settlement of the Promised Land. This volume begins with the exploits of Joshua, Moses' successor, and recounts in epic form the battles he fought and won.

After Joshua we read about the judges, heroes and heroines whose strange lives and deeds tell us that God can choose anyone to accomplish his plans. Wars and turmoil caused the people to ask Samuel, the last of the judges, to give them a king. Reluctantly Samuel agreed.

The first of the kings, Saul from Benjamin's tribe, proved to be more successful as a military leader than as a king. After his death, a popular, talented young man — David, son of Jesse of the tribe of Judah — became king. David united the kingdom, making Jerusalem its political and religious center.

We know more about King David than almost anyone else in the Bible because during his reign scribes began to keep written records. David also wrote down many of his thoughts and actions in beautiful poems called psalms. These psalms continue to be favorite prayers and songs for Jews and Christians even now.

Many of the stories found in this book were passed down by word of mouth for centuries. In the telling of these stories the heroes and their deeds often became larger than life.

Archeological discoveries help establish a basis in fact for many of the events described, but accurate details were often not important to the story teller. What is important to the narrator and to us is, "What do the stories mean?" As we read, let's keep this important question in mind.

Catherine Litecky, CSJ

Moses, the Lord's leader and law-giver, had died on Mount Nebo, from which he could see the Promised Land to the west across the Jordan River. Now it was time for God to carry out the promise he had made first to Abraham, and later to Isaac and Jacob. The Lord would fulfill his promise through Moses' successor — Joshua, the son of Nun. The Lord said to Joshua:

"Moses my servant is dead; now therefore arise, go over this Jordan, you and all this people, into the land which I am giving to them, to the people of Israel." (Joshua 1:2)

1 At the Lord's command, Joshua and the people of Israel prepared to cross the Jordan River to the Promised Land. Canaan was a very small country within which the climate and land varied greatly. The Canaanites lived in separate fortified cities.

The Lord continued to instruct Joshua by saying:
"No man shall be able to stand before you all the days of your life; as I was with Moses, so I will be with you; I will not fail you or forsake you. Be strong and of good courage; for you shall cause this people to inherit the land which I swore to their fathers to give them."

Then Joshua commanded the officers of the people, "Pass through the camp, and command the people, 'Prepare your provisions; for within three days you are to pass over this Jordan, to go in to take possession of the land which the Lord your God gives you to possess.'" (Joshua 1:5-6, 10-11)

All the people responded to Joshua, saying:

"All that you have commanded us we will do, and wherever you send us we will go. Just as we obeyed Moses in all things, so we will obey you; only may the Lord your God be with you as he was with Moses!"
(Joshua 1:16-17)

What was the land like that the Israelites were going to claim as their own? Canaan was not very large; it was only 54 miles across at its widest point and about 150 miles long. The Jordan River, fed by the snows of 9,000-foot Mount Hermon in the north, wound and looped its way south from the Sea of Galilee to the Dead Sea, which was about 1300 feet below sea level. The area around the Dead Sea, the lowest point on the earth's surface, was barren and hot, while the region near the Sea of Galilee was green and luxurious. West of the ten-mile-wide Jordan Valley were the central hills, or highlands; and even further west was the coastland along the Mediterranean Sea. Canaan, then, small as it was, contained a great variety of terrain, including deserts, farmlands, and towering mountains.

Canaan's climate, though varied, in general had two seasons. The summer, which extended from May to October, was sunny and rainless; the only moisture came from the dew and the morning mist. The winter was the rainy season. The "early rains" began in November and softened the earth for plowing; the "later rains" in March and April were necessary as the grain ripened for harvesting.

Canaan was not a unified country. It was made up of many different fortified cities, each one with its own ruler.

2 Joshua and his people
set foot in Canaan
at a time in history
when Canaan was free
of the domination
of any great empire —
thanks to a people
called the Sea People.
They had first destroyed
the Hittites in the north
and eventually weakened
the Egyptians in the south.

At the time that Joshua was preparing his people to cross the Jordan, the two great empires that had controlled Canaan and neighboring Syria for centuries — the Egyptian and Hittite empires — were no longer very powerful. From about 1250 B.C. onward, both empires had been attacked by land-hungry invaders from the west, east, and north. The Hittite empire finally gave in to the attack, was divided up, and disappeared completely as an empire by around 1200 B.C. Egypt held on for awhile longer.

The invaders who destroyed the Hittites during the thirteenth century were a group known as the Sea People, because they traveled by sea. They came from eastern Europe, and they took over, one by one, the countries on the Mediterranean coast. In Greece they colonized the ter-

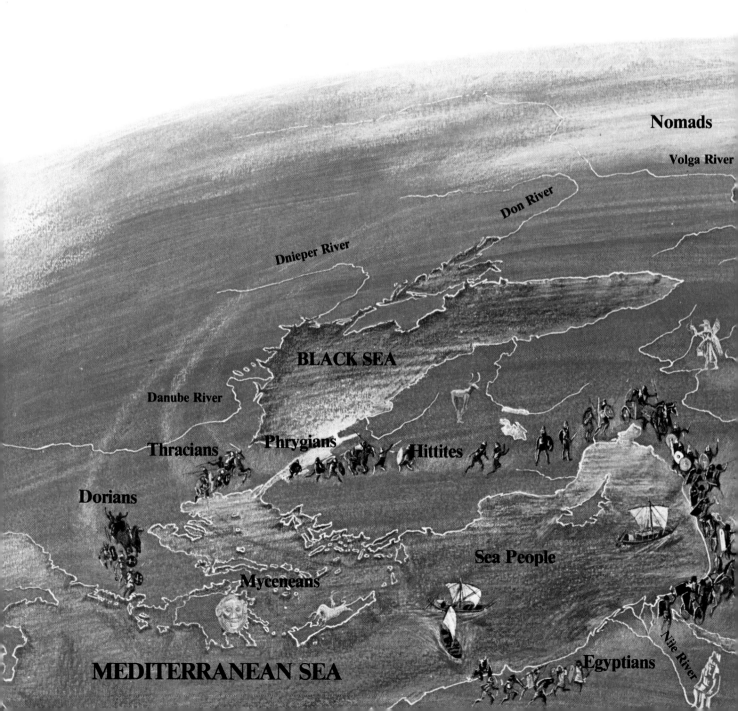

Nomads

Volga River

Don River

Dnieper River

BLACK SEA

Danube River

Thracians   Phrygians   Hittites

Dorians

Myceneans   Sea People

Nile River

MEDITERRANEAN SEA   Egyptians

ritories of the Achaeans, including Mycenae; they roamed over the Mediterranean Sea and landed in Crete, Cyprus, and Sicily. Eventually they even reached Libya and were at the gates of Egypt itself.

Pharaoh Merneptah succeeded in stopping the Sea People's further advance into Egypt for the time being, but he had other difficulties elsewhere. He was forced to send troops into Canaan to put down resistance to Egyptian rule. Eventually, under a series of weak pharaohs, Egypt lost its control of Canaan. Then a new wave of invasions by the Sea People — in both Canaan and Egypt — finished off Egypt as a great power. (A group of the Sea People settled along the southwest coast of Canaan.)

So, with the Hittite Empire carved up and Egypt greatly weakened, Canaan was free of the domination of others. This situation greatly helped Joshua in carrying out his plan of conquest. He was also helped by the fact that the small, independent city-states of Canaan were not united among themselves. Also, several Israelite tribes probably had already infiltrated into the more mountainous regions of Canaan — which were also the most sparsely populated parts of the land.

ARAL SEA

CASPIAN SEA

Medes

Persians

People of India

Tigris River

Assyrians

Elamites

Euphrates River

PERSIAN GULF

Israelites

RED SEA

3 Joshua's spies in Jericho
were saved by Rahab.
Later Joshua ordered the people
to cross the Jordan, after
the priests and holy ark.
The Jordan's waters stopped
so the people could pass over!

At long last, the land! The Israelites had been directing their steps toward this land for many years. And now that they were so near to their goal, how would they actually go about getting the land? Joshua's men were neither very numerous nor well-armed. They were going to have to be very clever. They were especially going to have to maintain their confidence in the Lord.

Joshua began by sending out two spies to check out the terrain ahead of them, particularly the walled city of Jericho. How could the two Israelites get into that city without being discovered? And once inside, with the gates closed, couldn't they easily be detected and captured?

Faced with this situation, Joshua's spies had an idea. After entering the city, they took refuge in the house of a prostitute, acting as if they had entered the city for that purpose. But the king of Jericho became suspicious. He ordered the prostitute, whose name was Rahab, to produce the two men. Instead, Rahab hid the men on the roof of her house and sent word that they had already left. Then she went up to the roof, and surprisingly, she spoke almost as if she were inspired to see the future. She said to the two Israelites:

"I know that the Lord has given you the land, and that the fear of you has fallen upon us, and that all the inhabitants of the land melt away before you.

"Now, then, swear to me by the Lord that as I have dealt kindly with you, you also will deal kindly with my father's house, and give me a sure sign, and save alive my father and mother, my brothers and sisters, and all who belong to them, and deliver our lives from death." (Joshua 2:9, 12-13)

Then, to prevent the two Israelite spies from being discovered, Rahab helped them go out a window and down a rope, after which they could escape to the mountains. Before they left, the spies told Rahab, "Put this scarlet cord in the window through which you let us down, and you will be spared, you and all your family."

The two spies returned to Joshua and told him about the city of Jericho and the people's fear of the Israelites. As a result, Joshua decided to go ahead and cross the Jordan River. The people were given this order:

"When you see the ark of the covenant of the Lord your God being carried by the Levitical priests, then you shall set out from your place and follow it." (Joshua 3:3)

The ark was given a place of honor because the Israelites believed that the Lord himself was the real leader of the expedition. The Lord was with Joshua, just as he had been with Moses.

Joshua assembled his people in a camp near the Jordan River, where they remained for three days. When the time came to cross the Jordan, a marvelous thing happened.

As soon as the priests stepped into the river, the water stopped flowing and piled up... and the people were able to cross over near Jericho. (Joshua 3:15-16 TEV)

Just as the Israelites had fled from Egypt, a land of slavery, by crossing the Red Sea, so now they entered the Promised Land, a land of freedom, by crossing the Jordan River. The biblical writers described crossing the Jordan River more as a religious procession than as a military action.

4 The Book of Joshua
tells the story
of the conquest
and occupation of Canaan
by Joshua and his followers.
After they had crossed
over the Jordan River
into the Promised Land,
Joshua ordered the priests
to gather twelve stones
from the river to set up
in the camp at Gilgal.
The stones were
in memory of the time
when the Israelites
crossed the river
on dry land.

Joshua is an early form of the name *Jesus*. It means "God is salvation" or "God saves." The name itself sums up the Book of Joshua. The book tells the story about how God saved his people while his promise made to Abraham was carried out. It tells how the Israelites took possession of the land of Canaan. The acquisition of Canaan was a test for the Israelites, a test both of their endurance and of their faith in God, who saves.

How, in fact, did the children of Israel take hold of their inheritance, the land of Canaan? The Book of Joshua says they moved in with one quick blow, a united people led by a single leader, Joshua. The Book of Joshua makes the Conquest sound simpler and easier than it probably was. It was a conquest, of course, because the Israelites really did have to fight in order to be able to settle there; the inhabitants of Canaan did not welcome the Israelites with open arms.

Throughout the entire story of the conquest of Canaan, the Bible makes clear what is really important: faithfulness to the Lord God. The children of Israel, even during the time in which they had wandered in the desert with Moses and Aaron, always ran the risk of being contaminated by the pagan customs of the peoples who surrounded them and turning their backs on God. Throughout their entire history, the Israelites had to fight against idolatry to remain faithful to the Lord. The various authors of the Book of Joshua, who wrote between 1000 B.C. and 600 B.C., were recalling that fact for their own later time as much as they were telling the story of the conquest of the Promised Land. A call to resist pagan influences is the main message of the Book of Joshua, one of the oldest books of the Bible.

This book assumed its present form some time after the rediscovery of the Book of Deuteronomy in 622 B.C. But the final written

version of the Book of Joshua is based on documents which are much older. Some of them go all the way back to the era of kings David and Solomon (tenth century B.C.), according to some scholars.

In other words, the writing of the Book of Joshua really was spread over several centuries. Some scholars believe six or seven principal authors were involved in writing it all down. However, the real author is the "God-who-saves." God is represented in the story by his lieutenant Joshua, the son of Nun, from the Hebrew tribe of Ephraim.

The Book of Joshua says that as soon as the Israelites had passed over the Jordan River, the Lord instructed Joshua to choose twelve men, one from each tribe. Joshua did so, and then he told the twelve assembled men:

"Go into the Jordan, and take up each of you a stone upon his shoulder, according to the number of the tribes of the people of Israel, that this may be a sign among you, when your children ask in time to come, 'What do those stones mean to you?' Then you shall tell them that the waters of the Jordan were cut off before the ark of the covenant of the Lord; when it passed over the Jordan, the waters of the Jordan were cut off. So these stones shall be to the people of Israel a memorial for ever."

The people...encamped in Gilgal on the east border of Jericho. And those twelve stones, which they took out of the Jordan, Joshua set up in Gilgal. (Joshua 4:5-7, 19-20)

These twelve stones, or steles, arranged in a circle at Gilgal represented the twelve tribes of Israel. The circle of stones was a symbol of the entire nation and celebrated the glory of God, who had intervened to help Israel conquer the land promised to them.

5 The Israelites settled
for a while at Gilgal.
During this time,
the Israelites did
several things that were signs
that they were
the Lord's special people.
They circumcised all the males,
and they celebrated
the Passover of the Lord.

Crossing the Jordan was an accomplishment, but the Israelites had many more tasks ahead of them. They settled temporarily at a spot between the Jordan and Jericho; they named the place Gilgal, which means "circle of stones." We don't know the exact location of Gilgal. But here no doubt the children of Israel lived the kind of life that was typical of a semi-nomadic encampment. After their journey, the Israelites needed to settle down for a while and devote more time to such daily, common things as eating, talking, resting, and praying.

The Bible mentions a significant religious event that took place at Gilgal: the first celebration of the Passover in Canaan. This celebra-

tion linked the flight out of Egypt under Moses with the entry into the Promised Land under his successor, Joshua. This Passover celebration also underlined the difference between the children of Israel and the surrounding pagan populations.

The Israelites had another sign of their religious difference from all other peoples: circumcision. (Circumcision is the removal of the loose skin at the end of the penis.) It was not by accident that the Bible stressed this particular sign at this time — the moment when the children of Israel ran the risk of being assimilated into the surrounding pagan inhabitants of Canaan.

When the people of Israel left Egypt, all the males were already circumcised. However, during the forty years the people spent crossing the desert, none of the baby boys had been circumcised. Also, by the end of that time all the men who were fighting age when

they left Egypt had died because they had disobeyed the Lord. Just as he had sworn, they were not allowed to see the rich and fertile land that he had promised their ancestors. (Joshua 5:4-6 TEV)

It was therefore necessary once again to see to it that the men of Israel were circumcised, as the Lord had earlier commanded.

Then the Lord told Joshua, "Make some knives out of flint and circumcise the Israelites." So Joshua did as the Lord had commanded, and he circumcised the Israelites at a place called Circumcision Hill. (Joshua 5:2-3 TEV)

The celebration of the Passover and the observance of circumcision were two important signs of God's special call to the children of Israel. They had entered the Promised Land as members of the Lord's covenant community. They were set apart from all other peoples.

6 Jericho, the first city that Joshua conquered, was ancient even in Joshua's time. Through careful excavation, archeologists have learned much about Jericho's history.

Jericho — a famous city several times destroyed and then rebuilt — has been a great blessing to modern archeologists. Careful excavations have enabled them to uncover the main outlines of the earliest settlements on what is today called Tell-es-Sultan, the hill of Jericho, near the stream of Elisha. It was this same stream that once watered the ancient town, creating a luxuriant oasis filled with date palm trees as well as banana trees.

Jericho, "city of the moon god," was built on the site of what might have been the oldest city in the world. According to modern calculations, a city was first built there as long ago as ten thousand years — about seven thousand years before Joshua. We get some idea of its age when we realize that Abraham and his family are closer in time to *us* than they were to the *earliest* inhabitants of Jericho!

This long history of habitation on the site of

Ramparts and a tower from a dry stone wall around ten yards high and nine yards thick have been dug up from a period of time dating from around 8000 B.C. Curiously, the top of this tower emerged out of a hole dug around it — so much had the level of the ground arisen in the course of continuous human settlement on the site. Also found at this level were many cut stone tools. This early city was destroyed by war, fire or a plague — we're not sure which.

Around 6000 B.C. another city was rebuilt on top of the old one. We know from the way they treated their dead that the inhabitants of this city were religious people. Tombs have been excavated containing many human skulls coated with clay and with their eye sockets fitted with shells designed to remake human faces — very interesting human faces!

The site of Jericho was abandoned for many centuries. Then around 3000 B.C. Jericho was rebuilt again. During this period there were again thick walls with ramparts; this time, however, they were built out of bricks, not out of dry stones. Much beautiful pottery has been unearthed from this time.

And then everything was burned to the ground. Once again Jericho was reduced to ruins.

Around 2000 B.C. the Hyksos, invaders from the east, rebuilt the city with a new type of fortifications. They used massive piles of stone on the outside of the ramparts, shored up by piles of earth on the inside. Life in Jericho seems to have flourished during this period, judging from the remains of workshops where cloth was woven and pottery making and basket weaving were common.

After that came the time of Joshua, around 1200 B.C. The old ramparts had been destroyed by then, so Jericho was no longer secure from attack. The city was not entirely deserted, however. Probably nomad tribes had settled there in order to take advantage of the water from the nearby stream of Elisha.

Even though Jericho was no longer the stronghold it once had been, nevertheless, the reputation of ancient Jericho was so great in that part of the world that its conquest was considered a significant step in the taking over of the Promised Land. Probably the biblical writers told the marvelous story of the fall of Jericho in order to underline the truth that it was God who gave the land to the children of Israel.

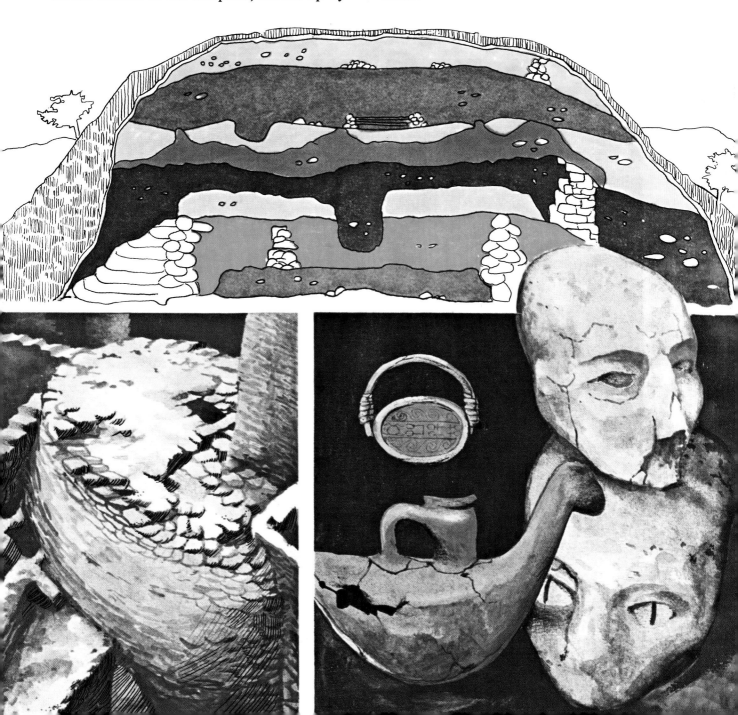

7 Amid trumpet blasts
and mighty shouts,
the walls of Jericho fell
to Joshua and his men.
The conquest of Canaan,
the Promised Land, had begun.

The Bible's story of the capture of Jericho is not intended to be a historical narrative in the sense that we today understand history. It is not presented in a factual, newspaper style. Rather, it is told in epic form — that is, presenting exact facts is not as important as getting across the picture of a great hero and people doing a great deed. The description of the battle of Jericho includes certain battle rituals, or common practices, that we find in other ancient accounts of battles. For example, the shout the Israelites were ordered to make during attack was a typical practice of warriors, intended to strike

terror into the hearts of their enemies. Also common was the blowing of horns. (These horns did not sound like the brilliant and high-pitched trumpets we know today; rather, they were rams' horns, which emitted low, mournful sounds similar to the bellowing of cattle.)

Let us, then, read the famous description of the battle of Jericho as the heroic account it was meant to be.

Then Joshua rose early in the morning, and the priests took up the ark of the Lord. And the seven priests bearing the seven trumpets of rams' horns before the ark of the Lord passed on, blowing the trumpets continually; and the armed men went before them, and the rear guard came after the ark of the Lord, while the trumpets blew continually. And the second day they marched around the city once, and returned into the camp. So they did for six days.

On the seventh day they rose early at the dawn of day, and marched around the city in the same manner seven times: it was only on that day that they marched around the city seven times. And at the seventh time, when the priests had blown the trumpets, Joshua said to the people, "Shout; for the Lord has given you the city. And the city and all that is within it shall be devoted to the Lord for destruction; only Rahab the harlot and all who are with her in her house shall live, because she hid the messengers that we sent." So the people shouted, and the trumpets were blown. As soon as the people heard the sound of the trumpet, the people raised a great shout, and the wall fell down flat, so that the people went up into the city, every man straight before him, and they took the city. (Joshua 6:12-17, 20)

The Israelites thought that the conquest of Canaan was a holy war, a war proclaimed and led by the Lord himself. One of the rules of such a war was that the Israelites shouldn't take any enemy goods or prisoners, because the victory belonged only to God. That meant that no captives could be left alive. Any Israelite who didn't respect this rule against taking booty or captives could be killed. The Israelites looked upon this harsh law of war as necessary to make sure that they didn't become contaminated by the pagan customs of the people among whom they lived.

There is another reason why the Bible emphasized that everything in Jericho should be destroyed. Around the time the biblical authors were putting the Book of Joshua into its final form, long after the time of the Conquest, the city of Samaria, capital of the northern kingdom of Israel, had been conquered by the Assyrians (722 B.C.) and the nation destroyed. Faced with this terrible event, the biblical authors wanted to teach their people this lesson: If the Israelites had only respected the laws of a holy war from the time they first entered Canaan, they would not presently have to be suffering at the hands of the Assyrians. Rather, the non-Israelites, such as the Assyrians, would have been killed off and would never have been able to master Israel as they were then doing.

8

Next Joshua, using
a very clever battle plan,
captured the city of Ai.
He tricked the king of Ai
by luring him away
from the city,
leaving it undefended.
Then a small group
of Joshua's men rushed
into the city and
destroyed it completely.

The conquest of the Promised Land didn't stop at Jericho. The Bible says the Israelites moved on, heading northwest; but first, on the way, they captured the city of Ai. Although capturing Ai was the logical next step for them, we don't know in precise detail just how the entire conquest of Canaan was managed.

Like the story of Jericho's capture, the heroic story of the capture of Ai was more like a marvelous tale than it was an exact historical account. In fact, the story seems to have been composed later on in order to explain the settlement of the tribe of Benjamin in the region around Ai. The story also provided a chance to talk about the bravery of the Israelites and the military skills of Joshua. Joshua was presented as a military commander of genius. Just consider this marvelous battle plan:

He took about five thousand men and put them in hiding west of the city, between Ai and Bethel. The soldiers were arranged for battle with the main camp north of the city and the rest of the men to the west. Joshua spent the night in the valley. When the king of Ai saw Joshua's men, he acted quickly. He and all his men went out toward the Jordan Valley to fight the Israelites at the same place as before, not knowing that he was about to be attacked from the rear. Joshua and his men pretended that they were retreating, and ran away toward the barren country. All the men in the city had been called together to go after them, and as they pursued Joshua, they kept getting farther away from the city. Every man in Ai went after the Israelites, and the city was left wide open, with no one to defend it.

Then the Lord said to Joshua, "Point your spear at Ai; I am giving it to you." Joshua did as he was told, and as soon as he lifted his hand, the men who had been hiding got up quickly, ran into the city and captured it. They immediately set the city on fire.

The Israelites killed every one of the enemy in the barren country where they had chased them. Then they went back to Ai and killed everyone there. Joshua kept his spear pointed at Ai and did not put it down until every person there had been killed. The whole population of Ai was killed that day— twelve thousand men and women.

He hanged the king of Ai from a tree and left his body there until evening. At sundown Joshua gave orders for the body to be removed, and it was thrown down at the entrance to the city gate. They covered it with a huge pile of stones, which is still there today.
(Joshua 8:12-19, 24-26, 29 TEV)

No one has ever discovered this pile of rocks. Some archeologists believe that Ai had already been abandoned by the time of Joshua. It's possible that Israel actually occupied this particular territory peacefully. The biblical authors who told this story stressed how completely Ai was ruined in order to emphasize that it was the Lord who gave the Promised Land to the Israelites. Nothing could stand against Israel if God willed the victory!

9 After the capture of Ai,
Joshua gathered the people
on Mount Ebal, near Shechem,
to renew their covenant
with the Lord God.
As the people stood
by the ark of the covenant,
Joshua offered sacrifices
to the Lord
and read aloud
the commandments of Moses.

The Israelites did not conquer the Promised Land only by fighting battles. They also did it through religious ceremonies in which they recalled and renewed their covenant with the Lord. Under Joshua, the Israelites regularly held such ceremonies to celebrate their taking possession of parts of the land. The Bible describes one such gathering held by Joshua after Ai was captured.

Joshua built on Mount Ebal an altar to the Lord, the God of Israel. . . . On it they offered burnt sacrifices to the Lord, and they also presented their fellowship offerings. There, with the Israelites looking on, Joshua made on stones a copy of the Law which Moses had written. The Israelites, with their leaders, officers, and judges, as well as the foreigners among them, stood on two sides of the Lord's Covenant Box, facing the levitical priests who carried it. Half of the people stood with their backs to Mount Gerizim and the other half with their backs

to Mount Ebal. The Lord's servant Moses had commanded them to do this when the time came for them to receive the blessing. Joshua then read aloud the whole Law, including the blessings and the curses, just as they are written in the book of the Law. Every one of the commandments of Moses was read by Joshua to the whole gathering, which included women and children, as well as the foreigners living among them.

(Joshua 8:30, 33-35 TEV)

These two mountains, Mount Gerizim and Mount Ebal, towered over the ancient city of Shechem, which guarded the mountain pass. Shechem, in the center of Canaan, was an important place. Here Abraham built his first altar after arriving in Canaan, and here God first said to Abraham, "I give this land to your descendants." Jacob lived near there for a time with Rachel and all his household after returning from Haran. The Book of Genesis contains a record of an old agreement between Jacob's family and the people of Shechem. Perhaps that is why the city and its surrounding territory seem to have become part of Israel peacefully. At any rate, there is no biblical account of a battle in this area during Joshua's time.

Many, many years after Joshua's time, the Samaritans—a group of people who were of mixed Israelite and foreign blood—built a temple on Mount Gerizim dedicated to the Lord. They prayed there instead of going to Jerusalem, as the other Jews did. In the New Testament, Jesus surprised both Jews and Samaritans when he declared that the time would come when people would not worship God either on Mount Gerizim or in Jerusalem, but in their hearts.

10 Joshua was tricked into peace
by the clever people of Gibeon.
When five nearby kings united
against Joshua, the Lord
made the sun stand still, so
Joshua had time to defeat them.

The inhabitants of Gibeon, a rich Canaanite town about seven miles from Ai, heard about Israel's victories. They were afraid of being attacked and destroyed. Rather than risk a battle, they preferred to make an alliance with Israel. But they didn't know how that would be possible. Joshua would never agree to deal with them, they reasoned, because his aim was to take over the cities in Canaan, not to recognize their right to exist. That is why the inhabitants of Gibeon thought up a trick to play on Joshua.

And they decided to deceive him. They went and got some food and loaded their donkeys with worn-out sacks and patched-up wineskins. They put on ragged clothes and worn-out sandals that had been mended. The bread they took with them was dry and moldy. Then they went to the camp at Gilgal and said to Joshua and the men of Israel, "We have come from a distant land. We want you to make a treaty with us."

Joshua made a treaty of friendship with the people of Gibeon and allowed them to live. The leaders of the community of Israel gave their solemn promise to keep the treaty.
(Joshua 9:4-6, 15 TEV)

Eventually the Israelites learned that these people actually came from nearby. But since the Israelite leaders had given their promise, they couldn't harm the Gibeonites. Instead, Joshua made the Gibeonites become servants who cut wood and carried water for the people of Israel.

Kings of five other cities south of Gibeon attempted to resist Israel rather than make peace. They combined their five armies and marched north to surround Gibeon. The Gibeonites sent to Gilgal for help from Joshua. He marched all night and at dawn surprised the Canaanite (Amorite) armies.

The battle went on all day and Joshua didn't want darkness to come to protect the enemy. The Bible tells about the end of this battle in marvelous, poetic language.

While the Amorites were running down the pass from the Israelite army, the Lord made large hailstones fall down on them all the way to Azekah. More were killed by the hailstones than by the Israelites.

On the day that the Lord gave the men of Israel victory over the Amorites, Joshua spoke to the Lord. In the presence of the Israelites he said,
"Sun, stand still over Gibeon;
Moon, stop over Aijalon Valley."
The sun stood still and the moon did not move until the nation had conquered its enemies. This is written in The Book of Jashar. The sun stood still in the middle of the sky and did not go down for a whole day. Never before, and never since, has there been a day like it, when the Lord obeyed a human being. The Lord fought on Israel's side!
(Joshua 10:11-14 TEV)

Some days later the five defiant kings, who had been hiding in caves, became five conquered kings. Joshua had them put to death and hanged from five different trees. Only at sunset did he order their bodies taken down.

11 To the Israelites,
God caused every event
in nature, for
God was the supreme ruler.
Psalm 29 sings
of God's power.

Only the language of poetry can describe the great God of the universe whom even the cosmic forces of nature obey. Psalm 29, a song of great lyrical beauty, exalts the Creator who is in charge of all of nature, including its storms. This psalm isn't meant to be a scientific description of nature. Rather, it attempts to make us admire the creation and to move us to praise its Creator with our prayers.

Praise the Lord, you heavenly beings;
    praise his glory and power.
Praise the Lord's glorious name;
        bow down before the Holy One
            when he appears.

The voice of the Lord is heard
        on the seas;
    the glorious God thunders,
    and his voice echoes over the ocean.
The voice of the Lord is heard
    in all its might and majesty.

The voice of the Lord breaks the cedars,
    even the cedars of Lebanon.
He makes the mountains of Lebanon
        jump like calves,
    and makes Mount Hermon leap
        like a young bull.

The voice of the Lord makes
        the lightning flash.
His voice makes the desert shake;
    he shakes the desert of Kadesh.
The Lord's voice shakes the oaks
and strips the leaves from the trees
    while everyone in his Temple
        shouts, "Glory to God!"

The Lord rules over the deep waters;
    he rules as king forever.
The Lord gives strength to his people
    and blesses them with peace.
                (Psalm 29 TEV)

12 Winning victory after victory,
Joshua was turning
the land of Canaan
into the land of Israel.
The people thought that God
was their real leader
in battle and conquest.
The Israelites divided the land
into areas for each tribe.
Certain cities were set aside
for the priests of Levi's tribe
and for places of refuge.

Makkedah, Libnah, Lachish, Eglon, Hebron, Debir—the list of conquered cities went on and on. And it was always the same story: Joshua won the battle!

The Book of Joshua relishes its telling of this piling up of one victory after another. The stories of these "lightning wars" praised the new position of the people of Israel: Canaan was becoming the land of Israel. Apparently it was about this time that the name of the people was first given to the land. The name *Israel* appears in sources outside the Bible in 1220 B.C. This indicates that Israel was at that time a known people already established in their homeland.

Of course the conquest of so many new places didn't happen without violence, especially if we are to believe all the accounts in the Book of Joshua. This is how it reports the fate reserved for the kings of Meron:

And the Lord said to Joshua, "Do not be afraid of them, for tomorrow at this time I will give over all of them, slain, to Israel; you shall hamstring their horses, and burn their chariots with fire." (Joshua 11:6)

The writers of the Book of Joshua pictured God as the commander-in-chief of the Israelites' armies. God led them in battle and destroyed their enemies. This picture gives us a strange view of God—one that we do not hold today. Nor do we think of war as a holy act, as the Israelites who fought under Joshua did. Wars are fought by human beings who are responsible for their own acts of violence.

Following their victories, the Israelites had to organize their settlement in Canaan and take possession of their conquered land. They divided the land into twelve "districts," one for each tribe, so that each of the twelve tribes would have its own place. Moses had already begun such a plan of allotting lands and of partitioning them among the children of Israel; Joshua completed the process. Eleazar the priest and the heads of the families of the Israelite tribes shared with Joshua the responsibility of distributing the land by casting lots, particularly the lots cast at Shiloh. (Casting lots is something like the modern-day practice of flipping a coin.)

The tribe of Levi, the third of Jacob's twelve sons, did not receive any particular territory. Levi's tribe supplied the priests (and later on, the Temple servants) who served all of the people, so all the other tribes together provided for the material needs of the Levites. The Levites lived in special "levitical towns" and were given nearby pasture land for their flocks. The house of Joseph actually consisted of two tribes: the tribes of Ephraim and Manasseh, Joseph's sons. The extra tribe which came from Joseph took the place of Levi's tribe, and thus there remained twelve tribal districts into which the land was divided.

Some people were favored in the division of the conquered territories of Canaan among the tribes. Caleb, for example, had shown himself to be a valiant scout even in the time of Moses; as a reward he and his clan received the valuable city of Hebron. Caleb and his people, the Kenizzites, became part of the tribe of Judah.

Finally, some cities were set up as cities of refuge, where fugitives could flee and claim a right of asylum, the right to be protected from arrest and prosecution. This right extended even to those who had committed murder, if the act had not been intentional.

Dan

Kedesh

Rehob

Abdon

Naphtali

Rimmon

Asher

Golan

Zebulon

Manasseh

Hammath

Issachar

Ramoth

Taanach

Manasseh

Mahanaim

Shechem

Gad

Ephraim

Beth-horan

Jazer

Aijalon

Benjamin

Dan

Gibeon

Bezer

Judah

Reuben

Libnah

Jahaz

Hebron

Simeon

Eshtemoa

Kadesh

worship center

levitical town

city of refuge

13 When he was old,
Joshua assembled
the people at Shechem.
He asked them to decide
to serve the Lord faithfully.
The people promised
to be loyal.

When Joshua was old and his people had already conquered and settled down in numerous areas in Canaan, Joshua assembled all the tribes at Shechem. He gathered both those who had entered into Canaan with him and those who were already settled there. Having gathered together all the leaders of the people, the elders, the heads, the judges, and the officers of Israel, Joshua spoke to them very seriously, reviewing the entire history of Israel up to that point.

Going back to the very beginning, Joshua talked about Abraham, the father of the whole people; he spoke of the great Exodus from Egypt, and, of course, of the entry into the Promised Land. He spoke as though the Lord himself was speaking and Joshua was merely the Lord's mouthpiece.

Joshua's speech was of great importance. In it Joshua invited the people to decide for God of their own free will, to be always faithful to him, to choose him as the guide and master of their lives, and to obey and carry out his laws. Joshua reminded the people of their obligation to observe the laws and customs established by the Lord, and he gave them fair warning of the seriousness of what they had chosen:

"Now then," Joshua continued, "honor the Lord and serve him sincerely and faithfully. Get rid of the gods which your ancestors used to worship in Mesopotamia and in Egypt, and serve only the Lord. If you are not willing to serve him, decide today whom you will serve, the gods your ancestors worshiped in Mesopotamia or the gods of the Amorites, in whose land you are now living. As for my family and me, we will serve the Lord."

The people replied, "We would never leave the Lord to serve other gods! The Lord our God brought our fathers and us out of slavery in Egypt, and we saw the miracles that he performed. He kept us safe wherever we went among all the nations through which we passed."

Joshua told them, "You are your own witnesses to the fact that you have chosen to serve the Lord."

"Yes," they said, "we are witnesses."

"Then get rid of those foreign gods that you have," he demanded, "and pledge your loyalty to the Lord, the God of Israel."

The people then said to Joshua, "We will serve the Lord our God. We will obey his commands."

So Joshua made a covenant for the people that day, and there at Shechem he gave them laws and rules to follow. Joshua wrote these commands in the book of the Law of God. Then he took a large stone and set it up under the oak tree in the Lord's sanctuary. He said to all the people, "This stone will be our witness. It has heard all the words that the Lord has spoken to us. So it will be a witness against you, to keep you from rebelling against your God." Then Joshua sent the people away, and everyone returned to his own part of the land.

After that, the Lord's servant Joshua son of Nun died at the age of a hundred and ten. They buried him on his own land at Timnath Serah in the hill country of Ephraim north of Mount Gaash. (Joshua 24:14-17, 22-30 TEV)

14

In Israel, the 200-year-period that followed Joshua's death was the period of the judges. The Israelites lived among the Canaanites and learned about their principal gods — El, Baal, and Astarte — and about their religious practices.

Joshua, the great conqueror, followed his ancestors to the grave around 1200 B.C. The two-hundred-year period which began at that time is called the period of the judges of Israel. During this time the children of Israel came to know well the long-promised land in which they were now settled — Canaan, a land already many thousands of years old.

Canaan was a territory that had often been invaded. Jericho, for example, from its beginning around 8000 B.C. had several times been captured and destroyed, because this city was a stronghold which had to be taken in order to occupy the rest of Canaan. The city had experienced such invaders as the Hurrites from Asia and the Ammonites from Arabia.

During the Middle Bronze Age, between 2050 and 1550 B.C., a wave of invaders called Canaanites took over the territory. They were nomads of semitic origin who had come originally from Mesopotamia. And they were still occupying this territory when the Israelites appeared as invaders themselves.

These Canaanites were a very religious people. Among the gods they worshiped was the god called El. El was considered a supreme god, father of gods and people, as well as the creator of the universe; he was considered a unique being.

The children of Israel were not uncomfortable with this belief; in fact, they sometimes used the same name, El, to speak of their own unique God. Sometimes they even used the plural form of El — Elohim — in order to suggest majesty when speaking about God.

For the Canaanites, however, two other divine beings shared the honors with El; they were named Baal and Astarte. El, the supreme god, was represented as an old man with a long, grey beard, who was usually seated upon a throne with steps leading up to it. Baal was usually represented with a thunderbolt; he was a fighting god, often shown mounted on a bull; often he was shown also with a lance sharp as an arrow on one end, merging into the branches

of a tree on the other end. In this way, he symbolized both "thunder" and "fertility" at the same time. Fertility, however, was especially represented by the goddess Astarte, also known as Ashtoreth.

The Canaanites generally worshiped their gods and goddesses out in the open, in natural settings. All around the countryside were shrines set up to honor particular gods or goddesses. Many of the shrines were simply smoothed stones or pillars erected in the middle of groves of trees. Sometimes these places of worship, called the "high places," had altars or even simple temples.

Not only were a variety of pagan gods and goddesses worshiped in these "high places," but on occasion human sacrifice was practiced. The religious ceremonies sometimes included fertility rites in which temple prostitutes and priests engaged in sex acts. Both the human sacrifice and the fertility rites were far from the standards of the law of Moses. In time, the children of Israel themselves became contaminated by these Canaanite religious practices; they sometimes joined in the evil practices of their Canaanite neighbors. (Later, prophets severely criticized them for it.)

Although Canaan's coastline offered the possibility of fishing for its inhabitants, the Canaanites had turned away from the sea and moved inland, where they successfully cultivated the land. The land there was fairly fertile, especially by comparison with the arid deserts which surrounded it.

15 The Book of Judges tells about the time when Israel was ruled by judges, special persons called to lead particular tribes in time of military need. During this time, the Israelites still fought many enemies: the Canaanites who remained, as well as neighboring peoples, especially the Philistines. Violence was commonplace.

What happened in Israel between the death of Joshua around 1200 B.C. and the establishment of the Israelite monarchy around 1020 B.C.? This was a period of great change in the history of the people and the country.

The tribes of Israel had succeeded in establishing themselves in the land of Canaan, but many of the Canaanite inhabitants already there continued to fight against them. Many cities resisted the Israelite conquest and occupation, and sometimes they were aided by forces from neighboring countries. The Israelites had to fight wars almost continuously with the Philistines, who lived on the coastline of Canaan, and with such neighboring countries as Midian and Moab. There were also conflicts among the Israelite tribes.

It was, then, a period of unusual violence, and also a time of wickedness. Many Israelites adopted as their own the local gods, such as the fertility god, Baal, and the goddess of love and fertility, Astarte. The Israelite tribes were not united as a nation, nor were they faithful to their covenant with the Lord, renewed at Shechem under Joshua's leadership.

During this entire period of time, the Israelites repeated over and over again the same sequence of events:

— The people of Israel sinned; they worshiped idols and forgot the Lord.
— God punished the people for their idolatry by allowing them to fall into the hands of an enemy.
— The people repented and asked God's forgiveness.
— God then raised up a "savior" to rescue the people; during this particular biblical period, such a savior was called a "judge."

The word *judge* in English means an official who has the authority to try cases at law and pronounce judgments. In the Bible, however, the judges of Israel were military heroes who rose up out of the ranks of the people as men or women provided by God to help defend Israel against her enemies. These judges were political and spiritual chiefs who had authority over the people. They were believed to be gifted with special gifts of courage and wisdom. They were not, however, always holy persons.

The Book of Judges tells about the time of the judges. Of course, not all the judges mentioned there were of equal importance.

16 The Book of Judges tells
two stories that teach
about life during this time.
In the first story, Micah had
statues of household gods —
a practice forbidden by Moses.
In the second story,
a terrible crime was committed,
setting all the tribes against
the tribe of Benjamin;
without a king the people
did as they pleased.

The period of the judges produced a series of adventure stories — most of them involved with plunder, violence, murder, or war. There are two such stories at the end of the Book of Judges, one of which is a truly horrifying tale. These particular stories are presented as a sort of conclusion to the Book of Judges. In a curious way, however, they really serve as a good introduction to this whole troubled period in the history of Israel — before the establishment of the monarchy, or kingship.

These two stories were no doubt placed at the end of Judges because they were written later. They were written by writers who favored establishing the monarchy, so naturally the writers were eager to make things sound bad without a king. Nevertheless, the stories provide us with a vivid picture of the state of the country and of the customs of the people during the period when the people were without a king and were living under the leadership of the various judges who rose up from time to time.

In these two stories, we can easily see the misfortunes of a people without the strong leadership of a king. Throughout the Book of Judges is this sad refrain: "In those days there was no king in Israel."

The First Story: The Stolen Priest

Micah, a man of the hill country of Ephraim, was prosperous enough to have a shrine or altar for worship in his own home. But Micah was not an entirely honest man, because he had stolen eleven hundred pieces of silver from his own mother. She pardoned him when he finally returned the silver, but then she had two hundred of the pieces of silver melted down and fashioned into the little idols, or statues, that were venerated as household, or family, gods called "teraphim."

What Micah lacked, though, was a priest to officiate at the idol worship he had begun in his

home. Lacking one, he at first made use of his own son. Later, when a Levite passed by, Micah hired him to be the priest; the Levites were the Israelite tribe from which priests were drawn.

But Micah's household worship did not continue undisturbed for long. At about that same time, some of the clans of the tribe of Dan were looking for new territories in which to establish themselves; they were crossing the hill country of Ephraim going north.

These Danites also were looking for a priest. Coming across the Levite employed by Micah, they persuaded him to leave Micah, join himself to them and be their priest. He was only too willing to join them, and even helped them to steal Micah's idols. Micah was left fuming mad because the Danites were too strong for him to prevent their taking away his priest and idols.

The point of this story seems to be to show that during the period of the judges in Israel, some Israelites had adopted the Canaanite practice of having graven images, or statues— forbidden by the commandments the Lord gave to Moses. The story also shows that the Israelite tribes were not permanently settled but still moving about from time to time as they encountered difficulty.

The Second Story: The Crime of the City of Gibeah

A Levite living far back in the hills of Ephraim went to find and bring back a concubine of his (a wife of lesser rank) who had run away and had tried to return to the house of her father at Bethlehem in Judah. In the course of their return journey to Ephraim, they stopped at Gibeah, in the territory of Benjamin, where a generous old man invited them to stay the night. They were enjoying his hospitality when all of a sudden they heard some men beating on the door. The men demanded that the Levite be given to them for sexual purposes. The old man begged them to stop. (The story up to this point is much like the story of Lot in Sodom.) Finally, the Levite gave the men his concubine, probably to save his own life. (The biblical writer expresses no horror at his doing so.) They raped her and then killed her.

Confronted with such a violent crime, the Levite cut up his concubine's body into twelve parts and sent a part to each of the twelve tribes of Israel. He did this to arouse all the tribes of Israel against the tribe of Benjamin. There followed a war to punish the Benjamites, in whose territory Gibeah was. Eventually the tribe of Benjamin was rehabilitated, but not before it had been almost totally destroyed.

The editor of the Book of Judges, after recounting these shocking stories, concludes the book by saying, "There was no king in Israel at that time. Everyone did whatever he pleased" (Judges 21:25 TEV). The editor is suggesting that if there had been a king, these terrible events would not have happened.

17 The Moabites, who lived east
of the Jordan River, took over
some of the land belonging
to the tribes of Ephraim
and Benjamin.
Through a clever trick,
a judge named Ehud
killed the Moabite king.
Then Ehud called the Israelites
to battle with the enemy.
"The Lord has given us
victory!" he claimed.

For some years the children of Israel did what
was evil in the sight of the Lord. To punish
them the Lord encouraged Eglon, the king of
Moab, to make war on Israel. The Moabites
pushed west across the Jordan and took over
Jericho and other lands belonging to the tribes
of Ephraim and Benjamin. After eighteen years
of occupation by the Moabites, the people
prayed for deliverance, and God sent them a
liberator—Ehud, a member of Benjamin's
tribe.

Ehud was left-handed and very skillful with a
knife—and he had an idea. Armed with a
double-bladed sword, he went to King Eglon,
pretending he was coming to pay tribute, that
is, the tax which the Moabites as conquerors
imposed on the Israelites. Ehud got himself in
to see the king alone by saying that he had a
confidential message to deliver to Eglon.

Then, as the king was sitting there alone in his cool room on the roof, Ehud went over to him and said, "I have a message from God for you." The king stood up. With his left hand Ehud took the sword from his right side and plunged it into the king's belly. The whole sword went in, handle and all, and the fat covered it up. Ehud did not pull it out of the king's belly, and it stuck out behind, between his legs. Then Ehud went outside, closed the doors behind him, locked them, and left. (Judges 3:20-23 TEV)

The king's servants thought the king was just in his bathroom when he failed to come out of his locked private chamber. After a while, however, when he still did not appear, they opened the door of Eglon's quarters and found the king lying dead on the ground. As for Ehud, he had slipped away and rejoined his troops. Ehud the judge had slain a tyrant!

When he arrived there in the hill country of Ephraim, he blew a trumpet to call the men of Israel to battle; then he led them down from the hills. He told them, "Follow me! The Lord has given you victory over your enemies, the Moabites." So they followed Ehud down and captured the place where the Moabites were to cross the Jordan; they did not allow a single man to cross. That day they killed about ten thousand of the best Moabite soldiers; none of them escaped. That day the Israelites defeated Moab and there was peace in the land for eighty years.
(Judges 3:27-30 TEV)

Eighty years! This figure of two-times-forty was often used by the biblical writers to indicate a long period of time.

18 The judge Deborah and Barak, her general, led the Israelites to great victory over Sisera. Sisera ran from the battle, only to be killed by Jael as he slept in her tent.

Another biblical story that happened during the time of the judges of Israel had these interesting characters:

Deborah. Her name means "bee." Like Miriam, the sister of Moses, she was a prophet. She was also a judge of Israel, living in the hill country of Ephraim. She was accustomed to hold audiences under "Deborah's Palm Tree," between Ramah and Bethel, where people came from far and wide to consult her.

Barak. His name means "flash." He was an Israelite general from the tribe of Naphtali. In response to Deborah's call for men to fight the Canaanites, Barak raised an army.

Sisera. He was the war chief of Jabin, who was the king of Hazor in Canaan. The Bible presents Sisera as an heroic warrior at the head of an unbelievable number of iron chariots—nine hundred of them! Sisera and his forces were preparing to attack the Israelites.

Jael. She was the wife of Heber the Kenite, a friend of Jabin's. She was not Jabin's friend, however.

This story had a familiar theme: Because Israel had turned away from God, God had no choice but to punish Israel. The God who punished, however, was the same God who saved, using specially chosen persons as his agents. In the case of this particular event, God's choices were two remarkable women.

The Israelites, led by Barak, were stationed on Mount Tabor in the north of the country. (The biblical writer was undoubtedly exaggerating in his claim that Barak had ten thousand men.) Sisera and his chariots arrived in the valley of the Kishon River, below Mount Tabor. Barak was reluctant to begin the battle. But Deborah had more faith than Barak in God's willingness to intervene to save his people:

Then Deborah said to Barak, "Go! The Lord is leading you! Today he has given you victory over Sisera." So Barak went down from Mount Tabor with his ten thousand men. When Barak attacked with his army, the Lord threw into confusion Sisera with all his chariots and men. Sisera got down from his chariot and fled on foot.

(Judges 4:14-15 TEV)

(Later in a song about the battle, the biblical writer says that Barak's chariots got mired in the flood waters of the Kishon River, possibly by a flash flood. This explains why Sisera had to get down from his chariot and flee by foot.)

Sisera ran away to Jael's tent, where Jael let him think he would be safe.

Sisera was so tired that he fell sound asleep. Then Jael took a hammer and a tent peg, quietly went up to him, and killed him by driving the peg right through the side of his head and into the ground. When Barak came looking for Sisera, Jael went out to meet him and said to him, "Come here! I'll show you the man you're looking for." So he went in with her, and there was Sisera on the ground, dead, with the tent peg through his head.

(Judges 4:21-22)

19 The Song of Deborah celebrated
Deborah and Barak's victory
over Sisera,
general for a Canaanite king.

Nothing is more natural than to sing the joy of
a victory. After the Israelites' victory at Mount
Tabor, their joy exploded in a glorious song
celebrating the mighty deeds of the Lord (who
is always seen in the Bible as the one in control
of events). A stirring poem about the battle and
what happened after it, the Song of Deborah is
one of the oldest examples of ancient Hebrew
literature. It was probably written soon after
the event.

Listen, you kings!
   Pay attention, you rulers!
I will sing and play music
   to Israel's God, the Lord.

Lead on, Deborah, lead on!
   Lead on! Sing a song! Lead on!
Forward, Barak son of Abinoam,
   lead your captives away!
Then the faithful ones came
     down to their leaders;
   the Lord's people came to him
     ready to fight.

At Taanach, by the stream of Megiddo,
   the kings came and fought;

the kings of Canaan fought,
  but they took no silver away.
The stars fought from the sky;
  as they moved across the sky,
  they fought against Sisera.
A flood in the Kishon swept them away—
  the onrushing Kishon River.
I shall march, march on, with strength!
Then the horses came galloping on,
  stamping the ground with their hoofs.

The most fortunate of women is Jael,
  the wife of Heber the Kenite—
  the most fortunate of women
    who live in tents.
Sisera asked her for water, but she
    gave him milk;
  she brought him cream in a
    beautiful bowl.
She took a tent peg in one hand,
    a workman's hammer in the other;
  she struck Sisera and crushed
    his skull;
  she pierced him through the head.
He sank to his knees,
  fell down and lay still at her feet.

At her feet he sank to his knees
    and fell;
  he fell to the ground, dead.
Sisera's mother looked out of
    the window;
  she gazed from behind the lattice.
"Why is his chariot so late in
    coming?" she asked.
  "Why are his horses so slow
    to return?"
Her wisest ladies answered her,
  and she told herself over and over,
"They are only finding things
    to capture and divide,
  a girl or two for every soldier,
  rich cloth for Sisera,
  embroidered pieces for the
    neck of the queen."
So may all your enemies die
    like that, O Lord,
  but may your friends shine
    like the rising sun!

And there was peace in the land for forty
years. (Judges 5:3, 12-13, 19-22, 24-31 TEV)

Once again the people turned away from God. This time God allowed them to fall into the hands of the Midianites. The camel-riding Midianites oppressed the children of Israel repeatedly. Year after year, just as the Israelites were ready to harvest their fields, the Midianites would swoop down on their fields, steal their crops, and ride off before they could be stopped. Many of the Israelites took refuge in the hills or hid out in caves. Finally, in their distress, the Israelites turned again to God and prayed to be delivered.

A certain man named Gideon was beating wheat in a winepress using the jagged edges of a rock. He was trying to hide this milling operation for fear the Midianites would come and take his grain away from him. While he was busy at this task, an angel of the Lord appeared to him under an oak tree in the village of Ophrah, near Shechem, in the territory of the tribe of Manasseh. The Lord's angel said to him:

"The Lord is with you, brave and mighty man!"

Gideon said to him, "If I may ask, sir, why has all this happened to us if the Lord is with us? What happened to all the wonderful things that our fathers told us the Lord used to do—how he brought them out of Egypt? The Lord has abandoned us and left us to the mercy of the Midianites."

Then the Lord ordered him, "Go with all your great strength and rescue Israel from the Midianites. I myself am sending you."

20 For years the Midianites
raided the fields and homes
of the Israelites,
especially in Manasseh.
The Lord's angel called upon
a farmer named Gideon
to rescue the Israelites.
When Gideon asked for
a sign of his mission,
the Lord did
a marvelous thing for him.
Then Gideon asked the Lord
for one more sign,
and he received it.

Gideon replied, "But Lord, how can I rescue Israel? My clan is the weakest in the tribe of Manasseh, and I am the least important member of my family."

The Lord answered, "You can do it because I will help you. You will crush the Midianites as easily as if they were only one man."

That night the Lord told Gideon, "Take your father's bull and another bull seven years old, tear down your father's altar to Baal, and cut down the symbol of the goddess Asherah, which was beside it. Build a well-constructed altar to the Lord your God on top of this mound. Then take the second bull and burn it whole as an offering, using for firewood the symbol of Asherah you have cut down." So Gideon took ten of his servants and did what the Lord had told him. He was too afraid of his family and the people in town to do it by day, so he did it at night. (Judges 6:12-16, 6:25-27 TEV)

In order to be sure that it was indeed the Lord who was calling him to be the liberator of his people, Gideon asked for a sign:

Then Gideon said to God, "You say that you have decided to use me to rescue Israel. Well, I am putting some wool on the ground where we thresh the wheat. If in the morning there is dew only on the wool but not on the ground, then I will know that you are going to use me to rescue Israel." That is exactly what happened. When Gideon got up early the next morning, he squeezed the wool and wrung enough dew out of it to fill a bowl with water. Then Gideon said to God, "Don't be angry with me; let me speak just once more. Please let me make one more test with the wool. This time let the wool be dry, and the ground be wet." That night God did that very thing. The next morning the wool was dry, but the ground was wet with dew.
(Judges 6:36-40 TEV)

21

Gideon, the farmer judge,
called up a large army.
The Lord helped Gideon
to choose three hundred men.
They surprised the Midianites
in a daring night raid, and
won an astounding victory!

Gideon arose early in the morning, set up camp near the Spring of Harod, and there assembled an army. (The Bible story says Gideon's army was thirty-two thousand men, certainly an exaggeration.) The Midianites were camped down in the valley not far away.

The Lord said to Gideon, "The men you have are too many for me to give them victory over the Midianites. They might think that they had won by themselves, and so give me no credit. Announce to the people, 'Anyone who is afraid should go back home, and we will stay here at Mount Gilead.' " So twenty-two thousand went back, but ten thousand stayed.

Then the Lord said to Gideon, "You still have too many men. Take them down to the water, and I will separate them for you there. If I tell you a man should go with you, he will go. If I tell you a man should not go with you, he will not go." Gideon took the men down to the water, and the Lord told him, "Separate everyone who laps up the water with his tongue like a dog, from everyone who gets down on his knees to drink." There were three hundred men who scooped up water in their hands and lapped it; all the others got down on their knees to drink. The Lord said to Gideon, "I will rescue you and give you victory over the Midianites with the three hundred men who lapped the water. Tell everyone else to go home."

(Judges 7:2-7 TEV)

Gideon organized the men who remained and gave them orders. He divided them into three groups, and gave each man a horn and an empty jar, with a flaming torch inside the jar.

At midnight the changing of the guard took place in the Midianite camp. At an agreed-upon signal, each one of Gideon's men broke his jar with a loud noise, exposing his flaming torch. At the same moment each man blew on his horn and began to cry out, "A sword for the Lord and for Gideon!"

The result was absolute panic in the Midianite camp. Some of the Midianites did not recognize each other in the confusion, and they ended up fighting and killing each other; other Midianites simply fled.

After that, the Israelites said to Gideon, "Be our ruler—you and your descendants after you. You have saved us from the Midianites."

Gideon answered, "I will not be your ruler, nor will my son. The Lord will be your ruler."

(Judges 8:22-23 TEV)

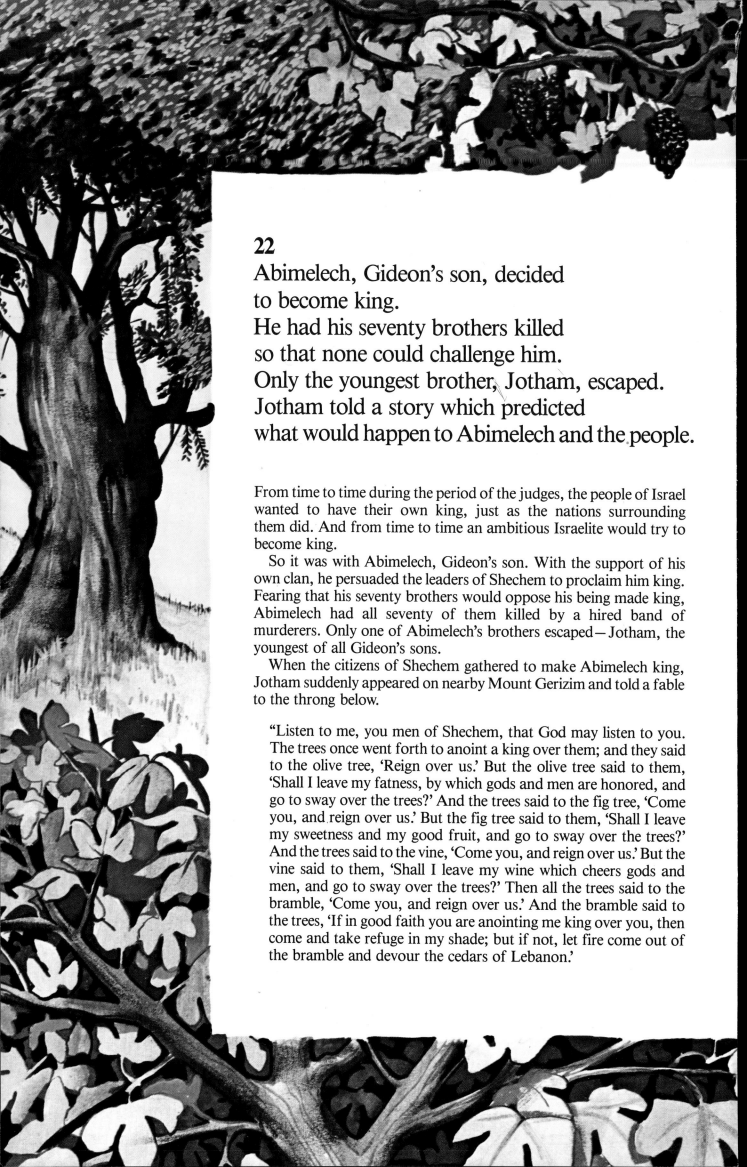

22

Abimelech, Gideon's son, decided
to become king.
He had his seventy brothers killed
so that none could challenge him.
Only the youngest brother, Jotham, escaped.
Jotham told a story which predicted
what would happen to Abimelech and the people.

From time to time during the period of the judges, the people of Israel
wanted to have their own king, just as the nations surrounding
them did. And from time to time an ambitious Israelite would try to
become king.

So it was with Abimelech, Gideon's son. With the support of his
own clan, he persuaded the leaders of Shechem to proclaim him king.
Fearing that his seventy brothers would oppose his being made king,
Abimelech had all seventy of them killed by a hired band of
murderers. Only one of Abimelech's brothers escaped—Jotham, the
youngest of all Gideon's sons.

When the citizens of Shechem gathered to make Abimelech king,
Jotham suddenly appeared on nearby Mount Gerizim and told a fable
to the throng below.

"Listen to me, you men of Shechem, that God may listen to you.
The trees once went forth to anoint a king over them; and they said
to the olive tree, 'Reign over us.' But the olive tree said to them,
'Shall I leave my fatness, by which gods and men are honored, and
go to sway over the trees?' And the trees said to the fig tree, 'Come
you, and reign over us.' But the fig tree said to them, 'Shall I leave
my sweetness and my good fruit, and go to sway over the trees?'
And the trees said to the vine, 'Come you, and reign over us.' But the
vine said to them, 'Shall I leave my wine which cheers gods and
men, and go to sway over the trees?' Then all the trees said to the
bramble, 'Come you, and reign over us.' And the bramble said to
the trees, 'If in good faith you are anointing me king over you, then
come and take refuge in my shade; but if not, let fire come out of
the bramble and devour the cedars of Lebanon.'

If you then have acted in good faith and honor with Jerubbaal and with his house this day, then rejoice in Abimelech, and let him also rejoice in you; but if not, let fire come out from Abimelech, and devour the citizens of Shechem, and Beth-millo; and let fire come out from the citizens of Shechem, and from Beth-millo, and devour Abimelech." (Judges 9:7-15 19-20)

Jotham's parable (a story with one main point) was meant to show the people what would happen if Abimelech, represented by the bramble in the story, became king. Abimelech and all his supporters would be destroyed.

Abimelech reigned for three years, and then plots began to be organized against him, and before long there were open revolts by the people. Abimelech used force to put down the revolts. While he and his army were besieging Thebez, a city near Shechem, a woman threw a millstone down from the wall on him, and it crushed Abimelech's skull.

Then he quickly called the young man who was carrying his weapons and told him, "Draw your sword and kill me. I don't want it said that a woman killed me." So the young man ran him through, and he died. (Judges 9:54 TEV)

And so this accursed king died. The biblical writer concludes the story with these words:

And so it was that God paid Abimelech back for the crime that he committed against his father in killing his seventy brothers. God also made the men of Shechem suffer for their wickedness, just as Jotham, Gideon's son, said they would when he cursed them.
(Judges 9:56-57 TEV)

Once again, however, God raised up a liberator of Israel: Jephthah. He came from the very region of Gilead that the Ammonites were trying to take over. Jephthah, the son of a prostitute, had been driven out by his half-brothers, who didn't want to share an inheritance with him. He had fled eastward and become the daring leader of an outlaw band. Not generally respected, Jephthah was called upon to lead the people only when the situation had become desperate.

Jephthah at first tried to negotiate with the Ammonites, but these talks came to nothing. War broke out. At that point, Jephthah made a strange vow: He promised to sacrifice the first person he met upon returning home, if God would grant him victory over the Ammonites. Jephthah did turn out to be the victor over the Ammonites, but he came to regret his vow bitterly:

> Then Jephthah came to his home at Mizpah; and behold, his daughter came out to meet him with timbrels and with dances; she was his only child; beside her he had neither son nor daughter. And when he saw her, he rent his clothes, and said, "Alas, my daughter!

23 The Lord chose Jephthah to drive out the Ammonites. In honor of his victory, Jephthah vowed to sacrifice the first person he met after returning home. Unfortunately, his daughter came to meet him.

Once again, Israel sinned by doing what was displeasing in the sight of the Lord, honoring and serving the pagan gods, Baal and Astarte. Once again, God allowed the Israelites to be delivered into the hands of the enemy—this time, the Ammonites. They lived across the Jordan in the region of Gilead, adjoining the territories of Ephraim and Manasseh.

you have brought me very low, and you have become the cause of great trouble to me; for I have opened my mouth to the Lord, and I cannot take back my vow." And she said to him, "My father, if you have opened your mouth to the Lord, do to me according to what has gone forth from your mouth, now that the Lord has avenged you on your enemies, on the Ammonites." And she said to her father, "Let this thing be done for me; let me alone two months, that I may go and wander on the mountains, and bewail my virginity, I and my companions." And at the end of two months, she returned to her father, who did with her according to his vow which he had made. She had never known a man. And it became a custom in Israel that the daughters of Israel went year by year to lament the daughter of Jephthah the Gileadite four days in the year.

(Judges 11:34-37, 39-40)

Of course human sacrifices were absolutely forbidden in Israel. The story of Abraham, who took Isaac to be sacrificed and was stopped by God, shows the rejection of this practice by the ancient Hebrews. Later the prophets Jeremiah and Ezekiel would denounce it more than once. Jephthah, however, had allowed himself to be influenced by Canaanite customs and those of neighboring peoples such as the Ammonites, who sacrificed their children to the god Moloch.

24 The Philistines, living along the Mediterranean coast, were Israel's greatest enemy for years. They had a very strong army.

The Israelites had barely completed their conquest of most of Canaan when another people, the Philistines, invaded and occupied the southwestern part of the country, the plain along the Mediterranean coast between Jaffa and Gaza. The children of Israel had failed to win this territory from the Canaanites. They no longer had much chance of taking it over once the Philistines had made themselves masters of it. (This portion of land came to be known as *Philistia*, a name which later became *Palestine* and was given to the entire land of Canaan.)

Where did the Philistines come from? These formidable invaders came from eastern Europe —across the Great Sea, the Mediterranean. Known as the Sea People, they had first settled on the island of Crete, and from there had invaded southern Canaan. They soon intermarried with the Canaanites and adopted the Canaanite language and religion.

The Philistines must have been a fearsome sight. The men were tall and rangy and clad in loincloths plated with metal; they were also equipped with breastplates and round shields. They possessed the latest in weapons and armor. Though the Iron Age was still in its infancy, the Philistines already had arrows, lances, and javelins that were tipped with iron. They even had war chariots drawn by horses.

The weapons and armor of the children of Israel, compared to those of the Philistines, were laughable. Some of the Israelites were still fighting with stone axes; only their best soldiers possessed bronze-tipped weapons.

The Philistines quickly organized the part of Canaan they had conquered into five districts, each one centered around a principal city— Ashdod, Ashkelon, Gath, Gaza, and Ekron. These five cities were the centers of Philistine life and culture. Ceramics, gold-working, and iron-working flourished in them. These cities were also centers of religion based on reverence for the dead. Offerings of food and drink were placed in the graves, and the faces of the dead were drawn on the coffin covers.

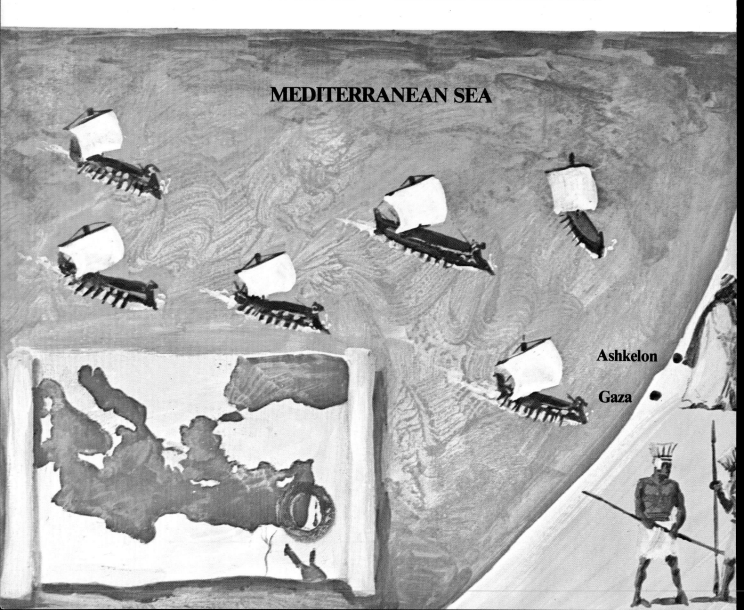

MEDITERRANEAN SEA

Ashkelon

Gaza

The Philistines worshiped three principal gods. *Dagon* was a harvest and fertility god, worshiped especially in the temples of Ashdod and Gaza. *Baal-Zebub* was a god whose name meant the "Baal of the flies." (In the gospels, the Prince of Demons is given this name.) He was a healer-god, and he was worshiped principally at Ekron. He also appeared among the Canaanite gods under the name of Baal-Hadda, the god of rain and storms. *Astarte* was a very well-known goddess of fertility, who was worshiped principally at Ashkelon.

Much influenced by Greek culture, the Philistines used in their new homeland all of the techniques they had learned in Crete. They developed the land of Canaan in a marvelous variety of ways. They were efficient farmers and fishermen and successful traders by sea. They were also skilled artisans as well as artists: they were famous as gold workers; their potters knew how to decorate vases and drinking pitchers with beautiful geometric designs. And above all, they were good soldiers, clever, resourceful, and well-armed.

Considering all these facts about the Philistines, it is not surprising that they were Israel's principal enemies up to the time of David the king.

PHILISTIA

DEAD SEA

The biblical story of Samson's exploits begins with a marvelous announcement: The angel of the Lord told the wife of Manoah, who was childless, that she would bear a child. From the time of his birth, Samson was consecrated to the service of the Lord. The spirit of the Lord was with him, giving him the strength he needed in order to be a hero of his people. As a sign of his almost superhuman strength, Samson let his hair grow long, and he grew up to be a powerful man.

25 The judge Samson married a Philistine woman, who betrayed him to her people. In a rage, Samson burned their fields and killed many.

The tribal territory of Dan lay next to the Philistines and fell under their control. The biblical writer claimed that the Israelites had fallen into the enemy's hands because they had been unfaithful to the Lord. After a time, God raised up a special liberator—Samson—who carried on a one-man war against the Philistines.

No one could guess this riddle. Samson's wife was annoyed because her husband would not tell her the answer. She kept after him, appealing to him in tears, until he finally gave in and told her the secret of the riddle. Almost immediately she told it to her countrymen. Furious at this betrayal by his wife, Samson stalked away for a time. When he returned and learned that his wife had been given away to his best man, he revenged himself upon the Philistines.

Samson fell in love with a Philistine woman. He insisted on marrying her even though she belonged to an enemy people. On his way to Timnah to get married, Samson was attacked by a lion.

Suddenly the power of the Lord made Samson strong, and he tore the lion apart with his bare hands, as if it were a young goat. (Judges 14:6 TEV)

Going back by the same path a few days later, Samson saw that a swarm of bees was living in the lion's body and were producing honey. This made Samson think up a riddle, which he presented a few days later to a group of Philistines invited to his wedding celebration:

"Out of the eater came something to eat.
Out of the strong came something sweet."
(Judges 14:14)

So [Samson] went and caught three hundred foxes. Two at a time, he tied their tails together and put torches in the knots. Then he set fire to the torches and turned the foxes loose in the Philistine wheat fields. In this way he burned up not only the wheat that had been harvested but also the wheat that was still in the fields. The olive orchards were also burned. (Judges 15:4-5 TEV)

The furious Philistines burned Samson's wife and her father, and so Samson attacked them, killing many. Then he went to life in a cliff cave near Etam.

26 Delilah told the Philistines the secret of Samson's strength. The captive Samson got revenge by pulling down Dagan's temple.

Samson later fell in love with still another Philistine, a beautiful woman named Delilah. Her fellow Philistines promised her a hundred pieces of silver if she could succeed in learning from Samson the secret of his strength.

Delilah questioned Samson closely, and he eventually told her, "If you tied me up with seven bowstrings, I would lose all my strength and be reduced to nothing." So the Philistines did tie Samson up in this way while he was asleep and then they hid.

Delilah cried out, "Watch out! The Philistines are coming!" Samson jumped up immediately and burst the bowstrings he was tied up with as easily as one might burst so many threads. Delilah scolded Samson for having fooled her and again asked him the secret of his strength. This time Samson replied, "I would not be able to resist if someone succeeded in holding the seven braids of my hair together with a weaver's

comb." This was done while Samson was asleep. But, again, he was able easily to free himself.

Finally, Delilah said to him, "How can you say that you love me? You keep on hiding from me the truth about what makes you so strong."

So finally Samson explained that he was a "Nazarite," a person consecrated to God. As a sign of that consecration, he wore his hair long. "If my hair were cut," confessed Samson, "I'd lose my strength and be as weak as anyone else."

Then Delilah lulled Samson to sleep upon her knees, and called in a man who shaved his head. His strength then disappeared instantly; God withdrew from Samson.

The Philistines captured him and put his eyes out. They took him to Gaza, chained him with bronze chains, and put him to work grinding at the mill in the prison. But his hair started growing back. (Judges 16:21-22 TEV)

Then one day the Philistines took the blinded Samson to a great feast held in the temple of the god Dagon. Samson was led to the Temple's terrace, where three thousand men and women were already assembled. Samson prayed fervently to God, asking for strength to revenge his enemies.

So Samson took hold of the two middle columns holding up the building. Putting one hand on each column, he pushed against them and shouted, "Let me die with the Philistines!" He pushed with all his might, and the building fell down on the five kings and everyone else. Samson killed more people at his death than he had killed during his life. (Judges 16:29-30 TEV)

27 When the Hittites discovered how to extract iron from ore, the Iron Age began.
The Philistines knew the secret but didn't tell the Israelites.

Living as we do in a world of supersonic jets, computers, and space satellites, we sometimes forget that humanity for most of its time on earth went without these and thousands of other discoveries and inventions. In order to appreciate the beginning of the use of iron in the time of the judges, let's take a look at some of the major periods in the history of human progress up until then.

The Paleolithic Period: the Old Stone Age, from earliest peoples up to 8,000 B.C. In this age people used implements of cut stone both as tools and as weapons. They began to cultivate crops and domesticate animals.

The Neolithic Period: the New Stone Age, between around 8000 and 4000 B.C. This was the period when pottery-making was perfected. City and town life began at this time, as did the manufacture of the objects that support this kind of settled social life.

The Chalcolithic Period: the Copper Age, between around 4000 and 3000 B.C. Metalworking began about this time, although iron had not yet been discovered.

The Bronze Period: an era lasting from about 3000 B.C. to 1200 B.C., known as an age of artisanship. Tin was discovered, and the alloy (mixture) of tin and copper known as bronze gave its name to the period. This new metal made possible the manufacture of chariots and armor as well as bronze sculptures. Horses were tamed during this period. The first form of writing at Sumer (around 3000 B.C.)

was followed by alphabetic writing in Phoenicia (around 1500 B.C.). This same brilliant age saw the development of gold-working and ceramics.

Towards the end of the Bronze Age, between 1400 and 1300 B.C., the inhabitants of Mesopotamia noticed a very interesting fact. They observed that whenever meteorites — considered "celestial," or heavenly, rocks — fell to the earth, they burned with a fiery glow. The Mesopotamians concluded that the meteors must contain some extraordinary element. That element turned out to be iron. But they did not yet know how to extract the iron from the stone in which it was embedded.

It was the Hittites in Asia Minor who finally discovered iron ore. They learned very quickly how to make good use of it. Once the Philistines, the Sea People, had invaded the lands of the Hittites, it was not long before they also knew how to extract and then use iron. It was with the help of superior iron weapons that they took over the Mediterranean coast of Canaan. The Iron Age was born.

The use of iron brought about a revolution in daily life. Implements such as iron ploughshares, scythes, and shovels transformed agriculture. The use of iron brought about a revolution in the military arts as well. Little wars fought with stone axes, polished stones, and flint arrowheads were no longer the same when enemies with metal armor were encountered.

It required time before all the modernization taking place actually reached Israel. Not until the reign of King Solomon (961 B.C.) did the Iron Age fully come to Israel. Up until then, the secret of making iron was kept from the Israelites by the Philistines, so that they would not be able to make swords or spears for warfare.

28

From the Canaanites, the people of Israel
adopted many ideas about settled living.
But the tribes were not united,
and they had no national army.
They began to want a king to unite them.

During the period of the judges, the still quite small number of people
that made up Israel worked hard at adapting to life in Canaan. The
children of Israel, once nomads, now lived in small cities — either conquered Canaanite cities or ones they established themselves. They
farmed the land which surrounded the cities. From the Canaanites the
Israelites learned how to clear fields, and then plow, seed, and fertilize
them. They learned how to terrace hillsides and what crops to plant.
Using slaked lime, they constructed water-holding cisterns under most
homes; in this way, they were able to withstand dry periods and were
also less dependent upon natural water supply.

There was, however, little unity among the tribes. Each tribe was
more concerned with its own problems than with those of its neighboring tribes. No central government with a king and a capital city

bound the tribes together. They were even divided by the geography of the land. The northern tribes in Galilee were separated from the others by the Plain of Jezreel, which was held by the Canaanites; the deep Jordan valley separated the eastern and western tribes; and in the central hills the rugged land divided the people into small, isolated units.

There was no regular national army, of course. In order to wage war, a tribal leader had to recruit mercenaries, or paid troops. Besides, these small armies were poorly equipped. The Iron Age had begun, but Israel still waged war with slingshots, stone axes, and even cattle prods. Only the best soldiers carried bronze swords and lances, which were inferior to iron.

City government was still very simple. Each city had a council of elders to decide its public matters. Business and commerce were still based mostly on barter; one product was exchanged for another. Payment was often made "in kind" because little money was in circulation.

A few of the sheiks, or tribal leaders, with larger herds could order rich purple fabrics for themselves or decorate themselves with jewels from Phoenicia. Most of the people, however, were farmers or shepherds who lived a hard, modest, and uncertain life. Most of the population did not know either how to read or how to write.

Worship was carried out in the home at household shrines and in some sanctuary cities such as Shiloh, Bethel, Shechem, and Gilgal.

The tribes began to want a national leader to unify them. They wanted a king like the other nations had. They felt that a monarchy was the only form of government that would allow the nation to develop. They wanted an army to drive out the Philistines.

29

Hannah was very sad
about being childless, so
at the shrine at Shiloh
she prayed for a child.
The Lord answered her prayer,
and she gave birth to Samuel.
Samuel was dedicated to God.
Two books of the Bible —
the First and Second Books
of Samuel —
are named after him.
These two books record
the close of the period
of the judges and
the beginning of the monarchy
in the land of Israel.

In the town of Ramah lived a man named Elkanah, who had two wives, named Hannah and Peninnah. Peninnah had borne children; Hannah was sad because she was unable to have any and Peninnah made fun of her for being childless. Hannah could scarcely bear it any longer, and one day she made a special trip to pray at the shrine of the Lord in Shiloh. Weeping bitterly, she prayed,

> Lord Almighty, look at me, your servant! See my trouble and remember me! Don't forget me! If you give me a son, I promise that I will dedicate him to you for his whole life and that he will never have his hair cut.
> (1 Samuel 1:11 TEV)

By this prayer, Hannah meant that her son would be a Nazarite like Samson.

While she prayed at the temple entrance, moving her lips silently, the chief priest Eli noticed her. He thought Hannah was drunk, and he scolded her for drinking too much wine. She explained to him:

> "No, my lord, I am a woman sorely troubled; I have drunk neither wine nor strong drink, but I have been pouring out my soul before the Lord. Do not regard your maidservant as a base woman, for all along I have been speaking out of my great anxiety and vexation." Then Eli answered, "Go in peace, and the God of Israel grant your petition which you have made to him." (1 Samuel 1:15-17)

Back at Ramah, Hannah came together with her husband Elkanah. Very soon she joyfully realized that she was expecting a child. When her son was born, she named him Samuel. After Samuel was weaned, Hannah returned to the house of God at Shiloh, and there she made an offering of a young bull, a measure of flour, and a skin of wine. Samuel was dedicated to the Lord and became a Nazarite.

30 The Song of Hannah
thanks God for Samuel,
Hannah's newborn son.
It also praises God,
who helps the weak,
casts down the mighty,
and is the source of strength.

Hannah's heart overflowed with joy and gratitude for the birth of Samuel. According to Israelite tradition, Hannah sang a marvelous song celebrating God's gifts. Some Bible scholars believe that the Song of Hannah was actually written after her time; for one thing, the song speaks of a "king" in Israel, and Hannah lived before the Israelite monarchy was established.

The Song of Hannah resembles the psalms. In ancient Israel the psalms were not poems or songs that just happened to be written by some-body; usually they celebrated some event that was important in the life of the people. What the psalms especially celebrated was Israel's faith in the strength and goodness of the Lord. Hannah's song celebrates the birth of Samuel and also God's kindness to the poor and needy.

The Song of Hannah was one of the inspirations for Mary in her song of praise, the *Magnificat*. In the *Magnificat*, sung after Mary learned she was to be the mother of Jesus, Mary said, "He has put down the mighty from their thrones and exalted those of low degree. He has

filled the hungry with good things, and the rich he has sent empty away" (Luke 1:52-53).

Here, then, is the Old Testament's Song of Hannah:

"The Lord has filled my heart with joy;
    how happy I am because of
        what he has done!
I laugh at my enemies;
    how joyful I am because
        God has helped me!

No one is holy like the Lord;
    there is none like him,
    no protector like our God.
Stop your loud boasting;
    silence your proud words.
For the Lord is a God who knows.
    and he judges all that people do.
The bows of strong soldiers are broken.
The people who once were well fed
    now hire themselves out to get food,
    but the hungry are hungry no more.
The childless wife has borne
        seven children,
    but the mother of many is
        left with none.
The Lord kills and restores to life;
    he sends people to the world
        of the dead
    and brings them back again.
He makes some men poor
        and others rich;
    he humbles some and makes
        others great.
He lifts the poor from the dust
    and raises the needy from
        their misery.
He makes them companions of princes
    and puts them in places of honor.
The foundations of the earth
        belong to the Lord;
    on them he has built the world.

He protects the lives of his
        faithful people.
    but the wicked disappear
        in darkness;
    a man does not triumph by
        his own strength.
The Lord's enemies will be destroyed;
    he will thunder against them
        from heaven.
The Lord will judge the whole world;
    he will give power to his king,
    he will make his chosen king
        victorious."

                              (1 Samuel 2:1-10 TEV)

31 The two priest sons of Eli
did evil in the Shiloh temple,
but Eli didn't stop them.
One night the Lord
repeatedly called to Samuel;
finally Samuel said, "Speak,
your servant is listening."
The Lord asked Samuel
to speak for him to Eli.
Samuel was the Lord's prophet.

The priest Eli had two sons who were also
priests at Shiloh—Hophni and Phinehas. But
they were not very good priests. They regularly
stole the food brought in by the people as offerings for sacrifice, and they also cooked it con-
trary to the laws of sacrifice. They even slept
with some of the women who worked near the

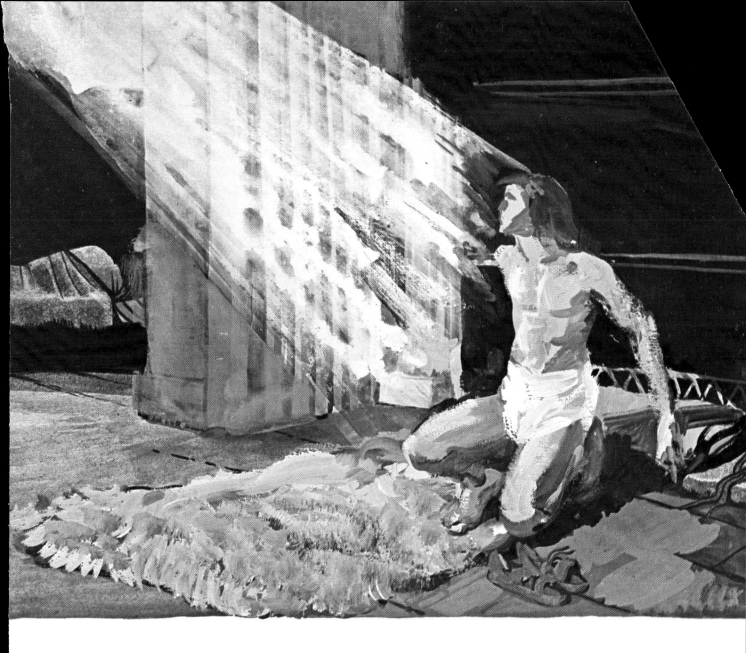

temple. Their father Eli was old and unable to make them stop their evil. Samuel, in the meantime, was growing and becoming pleasing— both to the Lord and to other people.

In those days, when the boy Samuel was serving the Lord under the direction of Eli, there were very few messages from the Lord, and visions from him were quite rare. One night Eli, who was now almost blind, was sleeping in his own room; Samuel was sleeping in the sanctuary, where the sacred Covenant Box was. Before dawn, while the lamp was still burning, the Lord called Samuel. He answered, "Yes, sir!" and ran to Eli and said, "You called me, and here I am."

But Eli answered, "I didn't call you; go back to bed." So Samuel went back to bed.

The Lord called Samuel again. The boy did not know that it was the Lord, because the Lord had never spoken to him before. So he got up, went to Eli, and said, "You called me, and here I am."

But Eli answered, "My son, I didn't call you; go back to bed."

The Lord called Samuel a third time; he got up, went to Eli, and said, "You called me, and here I am."

Then Eli realized that it was the Lord who was calling the boy, so he said to him, "Go back to bed; and if he calls you again, say, 'Speak, Lord, your servant is listening.' " So Samuel went back to bed.

The Lord came and stood there, and called as he had before, "Samuel! Samuel!"

Samuel answered, "Speak; your servant is listening."   (1 Samuel 2:26, 3:1-10 TEV)

Then the Lord told Samuel to inform Eli that he would have to be punished for not having corrected his wicked sons. This was the first task given to Samuel, who after that was considered a great prophet of the Lord throughout Israel.

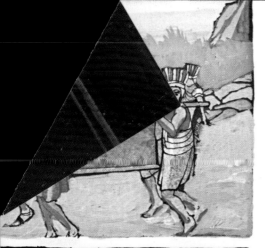

32

The Israelites brought the ark
of the covenant with them into battle,
and the Philistines captured it.
The Lord punished the Philistines
with a plague of tumors,
and they returned the ark.

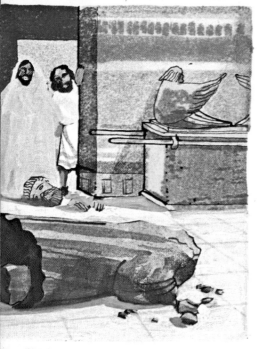

Sometime later, the Israelites and the Philistines fought one another in a fierce battle at Ebenezer. The Philistines soundly defeated the Israelites.

> And when the troops came to the camp, the elders of Israel said, "Why has the Lord put us to rout today before the Philistines? Let us bring the ark of the covenant of the Lord here from Shiloh, that he may come among us and save us from the power of our enemies." So the people sent to Shiloh, and brought from there the ark of the covenant of the Lord of hosts, who is enthroned on the cherubim; and the two sons of Eli, Hophni and Phinehas, were there with the ark of the covenant of God.
>
> When the ark of the covenant of the Lord came into the camp, all Israel gave a mighty shout, so that the earth resounded.
>
> (1 Samuel 4:3-5)

The Philistines were alarmed at the noise, though they did not panic completely. "Take courage and be strong," the leaders of the Philistines told their warriors.

The battle resumed, and the Israelites were again defeated and humiliated. The two sons of the priest Eli, Hophni and Phinehas, were

slain. But the worst thing that happened was that the ark of the covenant was captured. When old Eli heard this news back in Shiloh, he fell over backwards, broke his neck, and died.

The Philistines took the ark of the covenant to Ashdod, and set it up in the temple of the god Dagon, next to a statue representing that god. However, when the inhabitants of Ashdod came to the temple the next day, they saw that Dagon's statue had fallen face downwards on the ground in front of the ark of the Lord; the head and the hands of the idol were broken off and lying on the threshold.

The hand of the Lord was heavy upon the people of Ashdod, and he terrified and afflicted them with tumors, both Ashdod and its territory. And when the men of Ashdod saw how things were, they said, "The ark of the God of Israel must not remain with us; for his hand is heavy upon us and upon Dagon our god." (1 Samuel 5:6-7)

So the Philistines sent the ark of the covenant from city to city for seven months. But everywhere that the ark appeared, the same plague of tumors broke out. The Philistines then consulted their priests and magicians. They decided that the ark should be returned to the Israelites with a gift to their God, to pay for the sin of stealing the ark. The Philistines sent symbols of the plague, five golden tumors and five golden rodents, corresponding to the five principal Philistine chiefs.

Before long, some Israelites working in the fields near Bethshemesh saw a cart approaching. The cart, drawn by two lowing cattle, bore the ark and a chest containing the Philistine offerings.

The Israelites received back the ark in the field of Joshua of Bethshemesh. The Israelites there offered up the two cattle as a burnt offering to the Lord in thanksgiving near a place called "the great stone." The Bible records that God slew seventy of the Israelites because they were so bold as to try to look inside the ark.

After a number of adventures, the ark eventually was taken to Kiriath-jearim. It was from here that David would later move it to Jerusalem.

33 The people of Israel began to insist on having a king. Reluctantly, Samuel agreed. He was inspired by the Lord to go out to meet Saul, who was looking for lost donkeys. Samuel poured oil over Saul's head, anointing him king.

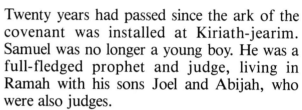

Twenty years had passed since the ark of the covenant was installed at Kiriath-jearim. Samuel was no longer a young boy. He was a full-fledged prophet and judge, living in Ramah with his sons Joel and Abijah, who were also judges.

At least once a year Samuel traveled to Bethel, Gilgal, and Mizpah to settle disputes among the Israelites. It was in Mizpah that he assembled the people of Israel for a solemn religious celebration, because the Philistines were once again menacing Israel. Praying to the

Lord, Samuel sacrificed a suckling lamb as a burnt offering. As he did so, the Lord unleashed a violent thunderstorm upon the Philistines, and the Israelites managed to stop their enemy.

After this victory at Mizpah, the Israelites were free of the Philistines for a time, but still they clamored for a king to lead them. This desire displeased Samuel, since he believed that Israel did not need any other king but the Lord. He was willing to go along with the idea of a king for Israel only after the Lord told him:

"Hearken to the voice of the people in all that they say to you; for they have not rejected you, but they have rejected me from being king over them." (1 Samuel 8:7)

Israel still had to decide how to choose a suitable king.

At that time in Israel there was a man of the tribe of Benjamin whose name was Kish. He had a son named Saul, a handsome young man a head taller than the other Israelites. One day some of Kish's donkeys ran away. He sent Saul, accompanied by one of the household servants, to look for them. Saul and the servant went from village to village, but they did not succeed in locating the lost animals.

When they arrived in the town of Zuph, Kish's servant suggested to Saul that he should consult one of the seers who was famous in the area. Some girls whom they met pointed the way to this seer's house. The seer was none other than Samuel himself.

Samuel had a premonition from the Lord that Saul would be visiting him, so he went out to meet Saul and invited him to come back to his house. He reassured him that he would find his father's lost animals; then he served him a good leg of lamb to eat. Afterwards, Saul passed a restful night on Samuel's terrace, and the next day Samuel accompanied Saul to the edge of town:

As they were going down to the outskirts of the city, Samuel said to Saul, "Tell the servant to pass on before us, and when he has passed on stop here yourself for a while, that I may make known to you the word of God."

Then Samuel took a vial of oil and poured it on his head, and kissed him and said, "Has not the Lord anointed you to be prince over his people? And you shall reign over the people of the Lord and you will save them from the hand of their enemies round about."

(1 Samuel 9:27; 10:1)

34 According to the Bible's
second story about
how Saul was chosen
to be Israel's king,
Saul was selected at Mizpah
by the casting of lots.
Samuel announced,
"This is the man
the Lord has chosen!"
Soon after Saul became king,
he raised a large army
and defeated the Ammonites.
Once more the people
proclaimed Saul king.

Two different versions about how Saul became
the king of Israel are recorded in the Bible. In
the last chapter, we read one of these stories, the
one in which Samuel anointed Saul with oil.
(Anointing with oil made an object or person
sacred.)

The second story in the Bible begins with
Samuel calling the people together at Mizpah
for a religious gathering. When they had
assembled, he said to them,

> "The Lord, the God of Israel, says, 'I
> brought you out of Egypt and rescued you
> from the Egyptians and all the other peoples
> who were oppressing you. I am your God,
> the one who rescues you from all your
> troubles and difficulties, but today you have
> rejected me and have asked me to give you a
> king. Very well, then, gather yourselves
> before the Lord by tribes and by clans.' "
> (1 Samuel 10:18-19 TEV)

Samuel then proceeded to select a candidate
by casting lots until every tribe, clan, and person was eliminated except the one the Lord

wanted to be ruler. Each tribe had representatives present. In the end, the lot fell to one of the smallest of the tribes, the tribe of Benjamin. Within the tribe of Benjamin, the lot fell to one of the least significant families, the clan of Matrites. Within this family, it was the tallest of the men to whom the lot fell: Saul. At that point, Saul hid himself among some baggage, perhaps because he was afraid or shy, but he was so tall that he could not escape being discovered. Then it was that Samuel said to him:

"Here is the man the Lord has chosen! There is no one else among us like him."

All the people shouted, "Long live the king!"

Samuel explained to the people the rights and duties of a king, and then wrote them in a book, which he deposited in a holy place. Then he sent everyone home. Saul also went back home to Gibeah. Some powerful men, whose hearts God had touched, went with him. But some worthless people said, "How can this fellow do us any good?" They despised Saul and did not bring him any gifts. (1 Samuel 10:24-27 TEV)

From the very beginning of Saul's reign, there was opposition to him.

Even after he became king, Saul continued to live a simple life as a farmer who tilled the land near Gibeah. One day about a month later, he was returning from his fields behind the oxen that he drove. Some messengers came to tell him that the neighboring Ammonites were provoking quarrels and fights with his people at the town of Jabesh. Saul immediately set about raising a large army, even though some tribes were reluctant. (The Bible speaks of 300,000 men in this army, an exaggeration, probably in order to underline the importance of the event.) Saul reviewed all his troops and at dawn led them into the battle. By noon he had won this battle, distinguishing himself greatly in the eyes of his comrades and his enemies.

Samuel said to them, "Let us all go to Gilgal and once more proclaim Saul as our king." So they all went to Gilgal, and there at the holy place they proclaimed Saul king. They offered fellowship sacrifices, and Saul and all the people of Israel celebrated the event. (1 Samuel 11:14-15 TEV)

35 Samuel worried about Israel's
having an earthly king;
the Lord was their real king.
Samuel warned the people
about their future with a king:
Their sons would be forced
into the army;
everyone would end up
working for the king
and giving him
the products of the field;
the people's precious freedom
would be taken away.

The Bible makes it very clear that the Israelite people's demand for a king went against Samuel's beliefs. Samuel thought the establishment of the monarchy would be an insult to God. After all, God already *was* the people's king, on earth as well as in heaven. How could they be so ungrateful to their wise and merciful Lord?

The Bible says that the Lord told Samuel to warn the people about the dangers of having a king. When we read the words the biblical author puts into Samuel's mouth regarding kingship, we should remember that these biblical texts about Samuel and his time were written down much later, some of them by writers who were very much against the monarchy. Also we should realize that another part of the Israelites' tradition speaks very favorably of kings, saying that the king was the anointed one, chosen by God himself.

Here is what Samuel tells the people about what it will be like to have a king.

"He will make soldiers of your sons; some of them will serve in his war chariots, others in his cavalry, and others will run before his chariots. He will make some of them officers in charge of a thousand men, and others in charge of fifty men. Your sons will have to plow his fields, harvest his crops, and make his weapons and the equipment for his chariots. Your daughters will have to make perfumes for him and work as his cooks and his bakers. He will take your best fields, vineyards, and olive groves, and give them to his officials. He will take a tenth of your grain and of your grapes for his court officers and other officials. He will take your servants and your best cattle and donkeys, and make them work for him. He will take a tenth of your flocks. And you yourselves will become his slaves. When that time comes, you will complain bitterly because of your king, whom you yourselves chose, but the Lord will not listen to your complaints."

(1 Samuel 8:11-18 TEV)

At another time, at Gilgal after the Ammonites had been destroyed, Samuel again voiced his worries about the kingship. This time the people grew worried, too. Samuel said,

"All will go well with you if you honor the Lord your God, serve him, listen to him, and obey his commands, and if you and your king follow him. But if you do not listen to the Lord but disobey his commands, he will be against you and your king. So then, stand where you are, and you will see the great thing which the Lord is going to do. It's the dry season, isn't it? But I will pray, and the Lord will send thunder and rain. When this happens, you will realize that you committed a great sin against the Lord when you asked him for a king."

So Samuel prayed, and on that same day the Lord sent thunder and rain. Then all the people became afraid of the Lord and of Samuel, and they said to Samuel, "Please, sir, pray to the Lord your God for us, so that we won't die. We now realize that, besides all our other sins, we have sinned by asking for a king."

"Don't be afraid," Samuel answered. "Even though you have done such an evil thing, do not turn away from the Lord, but serve him with all your heart. Don't go after false gods; they cannot help or save you, for they are not real. The Lord has made a solemn promise, and he will not abandon you, for he has decided to make you his own people." (1 Samuel 12:14-22 TEV)

36 Rather than wait any longer
for Samuel to come to offer
a sacrifice before battle, Saul
performed the sacrifice.
When Samuel arrived, he
grew very angry at Saul.
Even though Saul later won
victories over the Philistines,
he never again enjoyed
the prophet Samuel's support.

During the time when Samuel was judge, the
Israelites enjoyed more peace than they had
known previously. Unfortunately, this peace
did not last, for the Philistine danger was still
present. King Saul's reign was troubled from
the beginning. No sooner was he victorious
over the Ammonites than he had to face the
"hereditary enemy," the Philistines.

Saul's son Jonathan had become famous
when he killed the leader of the Philistines at
Geba. Saul decided to take advantage of this
victory by continuing a campaign against the
enemy. He called his people to war by sending a
messenger with a trumpet throughout the land;
the messenger called the people to join Saul at
Gilgal.

The Philistines assembled to fight the Israelites; they had thirty thousand war chariots,
six thousand horsemen, and as many soldiers
as there are grains of sand on the seashore.
They went to Michmash, east of Bethaven,
and camped there. Then they launched a
strong attack against the Israelites, putting
them in a desperate situation. Some of the
Israelites hid in caves and holes or among the
rocks or in pits and wells.

(1 Samuel 13:5-6 TEV)

Saul was still at Gilgal. The people with him there were terrified, and Saul was anxious to begin the battle. But it had been agreed that Samuel would come to sacrifice the customary burnt offering before the battle.

Samuel, however, continued to be delayed; seven days passed. Saul became so impatient that he finally decided to offer the sacrifice himself without waiting for Samuel. Samuel arrived while Saul was sacrificing. He became furious at Saul, who was not a priest, for daring to perform the sacrifice.

"What have you done?" And Saul said, "When I saw that the people were scattering from me, and that you did not come within the days appointed, and that the Philistines had mustered at Michmash, I said, 'Now the Philistines will come down upon me at Gilgal, and I have not entreated the favor of the Lord'; so I forced myself, and offered the burnt offering." And Samuel said to Saul, "You have done foolishly; you have not kept the commandment of the Lord your God, which he commanded you; for now the Lord would have established your kingdom over Israel for ever. But now your kingdom shall not continue; the Lord has sought out a man after his own heart; and the Lord has appointed him to be prince over his people, because you have not kept what the Lord commanded you." (1 Samuel 13:11-14)

Eventually Saul enjoyed victory over the Philistines at Michmash. They were thrown out of the central mountain territory and driven back to their coastal cities. The Israelites also managed to learn the secret of extracting iron from ore and were then able to forge stronger, better weapons and tools for themselves.

But with the incident at Gilgal, shadows had fallen over Saul's reign. It was the beginning of lasting trouble between the king and the prophet, the one who spoke for God.

37 Saul and his troops marched
south to fight the Amalekites.
Saul did not obey the rule
of "holy war" — to destroy all
property and persons captured.
As a result, Samuel once more
became angry at Saul and
completely rejected him.

After Saul had pushed back the Philistines at
Michmash, he marched south to the Negeb
desert to attack the nomadic tribes of the
Amalekites. The people of Israel had held a
grudge against the Amalekites from the time of
Moses on, because they had refused the mi-
grating Israelites the right to pass across their
territory.

The author of the Book of Samuel puts
awful words into the mouth of the Lord on the
subject of the Amalekites:

> "Go and attack the Amalekites and com-
> pletely destroy everything they have. Don't
> leave a thing; kill all the men, women,
> children, and babies; the cattle, sheep,
> camels, and donkeys." (1 Samuel 15:3 TEV)

The "sacred curse," or interdict, was the law of
holy wars which decreed that all booty — both
humans and property — taken in war had to be
destroyed and in this way offered up to the
Lord.

> Saul defeated the Amalekites, fighting all the
> way from Havilah to Shur, east of Egypt; he
> captured King Agag of Amalek alive and
> killed all the people. But Saul and his men
> spared Agag's life and did not kill the best
> sheep and cattle, the best calves and lambs,
> or anything else that was good; they de-
> stroyed only what was useless or worthless.
> (1 Samuel 15:7-9 TEV)

Samuel and Saul had two opposing ideas
about war. For Samuel, any war in which Israel
was involved had to be a "holy war." Any

peoples who fought the Israelites, the chosen people of God, were fighting God as well. What was captured in such a war could not, then, be kept by the Israelites; it must be destroyed because it was God's, not theirs. For Saul, war was simply a political action among peoples, rather than a "sacred" action. Consequently, there was no need to respect any "sacred curse," or interdict.

Samuel went up to Saul, who greeted him, saying, "The Lord bless you, Samuel! I have obeyed the Lord's command."

Samuel asked, "Why, then, do I hear cattle mooing and sheep bleating?"

Saul answered, "My men took them from the Amalekites. They kept the best sheep and cattle to offer as a sacrifice to the Lord your God, and the rest we have destroyed completely." (1 Samuel 15:13-15 TEV)

Samuel was very angry at Saul for disobeying the law of holy war. Even when Saul admitted his guilt and begged forgiveness, Samuel refused to listen. He told Saul, "You rejected the Lord's command, and now the Lord has rejected you as Israel's king."

So it was that Saul, who had been chosen by God, ended up being rejected by God. As for Samuel, he did not hesitate to cut down and kill the captured King of Amalek, Agag, saying to him, "As your sword has made women childless, so shall your mother be childless among women." Samuel never saw Saul again.

38 Saul continued his troubled
reign for some years longer.
The Bible tells several stories
about how David,
the next king of Israel,
began to attract attention.
One story claims
that Samuel discovered David
among Jesse's sons
and anointed him right away.
Another story says that David
was called to court to sing
and to play his lyre for Saul,
who liked David very much
and invited him to remain.

The Israelite monarchy had a rather awkward beginning. Saul proved to be a bad choice; his throne would not endure. He was not, however, removed from his throne immediately. He continued to reign for some time.

In his old age, Samuel had the task of looking for yet another king. He felt sad about Saul, and the Bible account says the Lord had to prod Samuel, saying, "How long will you grieve over Saul, since I have rejected him as king over Israel?"

The Bible gives several versions about how David ended up as the next king. The first account stresses that the selection of David was a special divine gift. In this tradition, the choice of David is presented as a surprising development that couldn't be explained by the normal course of events. In this story, Samuel is directed by the Lord to go to the tribal territory of Judah, to the house of Jesse, who paraded his seven sons before Samuel.

Samuel thought that Eliab would be the logical choice. He said to himself:

"This man standing here in the Lord's presence is surely the one he has chosen." But the Lord said to him, "Pay no attention to how tall and handsome he is. I have rejected him, because I do not judge as man judges. Man looks at the outward appearance, but I look at the heart."

In this way Jesse brought seven of his sons to Samuel. And Samuel said to him, "No, the Lord hasn't chosen any of these." Then he asked him, "Do you have any more sons?"

Jesse answered, "There is still the youngest, but he is out taking care of the sheep."

"Tell him to come here," Samuel said. "We won't offer the sacrifice until he comes." So Jesse sent for him. He was a handsome, healthy young man, and his eyes sparkled. The Lord said to Samuel, "This is the one—anoint him!" Samuel took the olive oil and anointed David in front of his brothers. Immediately the spirit of the Lord took control

of David and was with him from that day on.
Then Samuel returned to Ramah.

(1 Samuel 16:10-13 TEV)

This account never explains how David managed actually to get to the royal court of Saul.

A second biblical tradition tells us another
story about David. In it, we learn that things
were not always happy at the royal court in
Gibeah. Saul was often depressed; he was periodically tormented by what the Bible calls "an
evil spirit from the Lord." The people around
him had the idea of calling in a minstrel to sing
and soothe the king's nerves in the midst of his
depression. Someone in the king's circle told
about a shepherd boy in Bethlehem who was a
remarkable young man — not only was he intel-
ligent, courageous, and friendly but he also was
accomplished in playing a stringed instrument
called the lyre. This shepherd boy was named
David.

David came to Saul and entered his service.
Saul liked him very much and chose him as
the man to carry his weapons. Then Saul sent
a message to Jesse: "I like David. Let him
stay here in my service." From then on,
whenever the evil spirit sent by God came on
Saul, David would get his harp and play it.
The evil spirit would leave, and Saul would
feel better and be all right again.

(1 Samuel 16:21-23 TEV)

Yet another biblical tradition claims David
first came to Saul's attention as a result of his
remarkable combat alone with the giant
Goliath. That exploit made David famous at
one stroke.

39 Goliath, a Philistine soldier
of great size, challenged
the Israelites to send someone
to fight him until death.
David agreed to fight him
and chose the weapon
he would use: a sling
and five smooth stones.

War with the Philistines was more or less continuous throughout Saul's entire reign, but one battle became particularly famous. The Israelite and Philistine armies had taken up their positions on hillsides on either side of the valley of Socoh in Judah. Israel was carefully watching the enemy when a huge warrior nearly nine feet tall emerged out of the ranks of the Philistines. The giant was outfitted with leggings, a breastplate, and a helmet—all made out of bronze. He was armed with a large spear, tipped with iron. This mighty warrior was Goliath.

Goliath stood and shouted at the Israelites, "What are you doing there, lined up for battle? I am a Philistine, you slaves of Saul! Choose one of your men to fight me. If he wins and kills me, we will be your slaves; but if I win and kill him, you will be our slaves. Here and now I challenge the Israelite army. I dare you to pick someone to fight me!" When Saul and his men heard this, they were terrified. (1 Samuel 17:8-11 TEV)

Now the three eldest sons of Jesse were soldiers in Saul's army. One day Jesse asked David to carry some provisions to his brothers in Saul's army and learn how everything was going. When David arrived at the Israelite camp, he too heard the challenge Goliath was hurling at the Israelites. David did not like

Goliath humiliating his people; he was especially concerned because Goliath's challenge was an insult to the God of Israel. David offered to fight Goliath, and finally Saul agreed.

"All right," Saul answered. "Go, and the Lord be with you." He gave his own armor to David for him to wear; a bronze helmet, which he put on David's head, and a coat of armor. David strapped Saul's sword over the armor and tried to walk, but he couldn't because he wasn't used to wearing them. "I

can't fight with all this," he said to Saul. "I'm not used to it." So he took it all off. He took his shepherd's stick and then picked up five smooth stones from the stream and put them in his bag. With his sling ready, he went out to meet Goliath. (1 Samuel 17:37-40 TEV)

Goliath was scornful of David's challenge.

He said to David, "What's that stick for? Do you think I'm a dog?" And he called down curses from his god on David. "Come on," he challenged David, "and I will give your body to the birds and animals to eat."

David answered, "You are coming against me with sword, spear, and javelin, but I come against you in the name of the Lord Almighty, the God of the Israelite armies, which you have defied."

Goliath started walking toward David again, and David ran quickly toward the Philistine battle line to fight him. He reached into his bag and took out a stone, which he slung at Goliath. It hit him on the forehead and broke his skull, and Goliath fell face downward on the ground. And so, without a sword, David defeated and killed Goliath with a sling and a stone!

(1 Samuel 17:43-45, 48-50 TEV)

Goliath had relied on his own strength, while David had placed all his trust and confidence in the Lord as the source of his strength. The victory was the Lord's!

40 David became very popular. He and Jonathan, Saul's son, grew to be dear friends. Saul, jealous, several times tried to kill David, but failed. One time, Michal—David's wife and Saul's daughter— saved David. Warning him of Saul's intention, she let David down out of a window, and then deceived Saul's hired killers by putting the household idol in David's bed and covering it over.

Everyone loved David. He was handsome and ruddy-faced, with sparkling eyes and a warm heart. After his victory over Goliath, he gained the admiration of all.

Saul's eldest son Jonathan became very attached to David and loved him like a brother. In order to show how devoted he was to David, Jonathan stripped himself of his robe and his other princely clothes—even his bow, sword, and belt—and gave them all to David. A great friendship, which the Bible called a covenant, grew up between David and Jonathan.

David was also attractive to the women of Israel. Once when Saul was returning from battle with his men, the women came out of all the cities of Israel, singing and dancing, with tambourines and cries of joy. They compared Saul and David in their song: "Saul has slain his thousands, and David his ten thousands."

Yes, everyone loved David. Everyone but Saul. He was suspicious of this young man who was now a celebrity, almost to the point of

becoming Saul's rival. In his anxiety, Saul became very jealous of David. Several times when David was playing on the lyre for Saul to help calm his nerves, Saul took a spear in hand and tried to pin David to the wall. Agile as a leopard, David escaped him both times.

But Saul had decided on David's fate. He assigned David several dangerous military missions from which he hoped he would not return. Instead, David's popularity grew when he carried them out successfully. Finally, Saul decided to humiliate David by promising him his eldest daughter in marriage, and then giving her to another when the time came. (The biblical author seemed to want to blacken Saul's character in order to make David look better.)

David's failure to marry Saul's eldest daughter was a stroke of luck for Saul's younger daughter, Michal. She fell in love with David, and this time Saul gave his consent to the marriage, on condition that David and his men would kill one hundred Philistines in battle. Once again Saul hoped David would be killed instead. But David killed two hundred Philistines to win Michal, whom he married. Completely exasperated, Saul resorted to even stronger measures:

> That same night Saul sent some men to watch David's house and kill him the next morning. Michal, David's wife, warned him, "If you don't get away tonight, tomorrow you will be dead." She let him down from a window, and he ran away and escaped. Then she took the household idol, laid it on the bed, put a pillow made of goats' hair at its head, and put a cover over it. When Saul's men came to get David, Michal told them that he was sick. But Saul sent them back to see David for themselves. He ordered them, "Carry him here in his bed, and I will kill him." They went inside and found the household idol in the bed and the goats' hair pillow at its head. Saul asked Michal, "Why have you tricked me like this and let my enemy escape?"
>
> She answered, "He said he would kill me if I didn't help him escape."
>
> (1 Samuel 19:11-17 TEV)

Michal was so afraid of what Saul might do that she boldly lied to him, saying that David had threatened to kill her if she would not help him in his escape. Once again, Saul had failed to get rid of David.

41 David fled to escape Saul.
Saul, while pursuing David,
fell into a prophetic trance.
David sought refuge with
an unsuspecting priest,
Ahimelech.
Later, the furious Saul
killed Ahimelech, whom
he thought a traitor.

After all King Saul's attempts to have him killed, David had no choice but to flee. He first sought refuge at Ramah. There he met Samuel and told him that he was being pursued by Saul. Then both David and Samuel hid out in some nearby mountainous caves, where a group of religious men called prophets lived. These men traveled the countryside, singing and dancing themselves into trances.

When Saul heard about David's flight, he decided to pursue him. But the spirit of the Lord took possession of Saul on the way to Ramah. He fell into a trance, tore off all his clothes, and fell face down just as the prophets did.

David escaped and went to Jonathan. Jonathan, finally convinced that his father meant to kill David, told David about his father's evil plans. The two friends wept as they said good-bye and swore loyalty to each other.

Then Jonathan said to David, "God be with you. The Lord will make sure that you and I, and your descendants and mine, will forever keep the sacred promise we have made to each other." Then David left and Jonathan went back to the town.

David went to the priest Ahimelech in Nob. Ahimelech came out trembling to meet him and asked, "Why did you come here all by yourself?"

"I am here on the king's business," David answered. "He told me not to let anyone know what he sent me to do. As for my men, I have told them to meet me at a certain place." (1 Samuel 20:42; 21:1-2 TEV)

David tricked Ahimelech by leading him to believe he was carrying out a special mission for Saul. Ahimelech, unaware that David had been outlawed by Saul, welcomed David and the men with him. Since David's men were famished and the priest had no other food to give them, he offered them the holy bread reserved on the altar. They accepted it and ate it.

Now a certain man of the servants of Saul was there that day, detained before the Lord; his name was Doeg the Edomite, the chief of Saul's herdsmen. (1 Samuel 21:7)

Later Doeg the Edomite turned out to be an informer for Saul.

David departed from there and escaped to the cave of Adullam; and when his brothers and all his father's house heard it, they went down there to him. And every one who was in distress, and every one who was in debt, and every one who was discontented, gathered to him; and he became captain over them. And there were with him about four hundred men. (1 Samuel 22:1-2)

And so David, hunted and condemned to wander from place to place, became the chief of an outlaw band.

When Saul came back to his senses after his trance, he learned from Doeg the Edomite that Ahimelech had given hospitality to David and his men. Saul was furious. He sent an expedition to punish Ahimelech. This unfortunate priest was not given the opportunity to explain that David had lied to him and that he was not really a traitor to his king.

Saul said to Doeg, "You kill them!"—and Doeg killed them all. On that day he killed eighty-five priests who were qualified to wear the ephod. Saul also had all the other inhabitants of Nob, the city of priests, put to death: men and women, children and babies, cattle, donkeys, and sheep—they were all killed.

But Abiathar, one of Ahimelech's sons, escaped, and went and joined David.

(1 Samuel 22:18-20 TEV)

Later on, when David became king, he chose this same Abiathar to be his high priest.

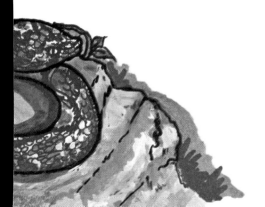

42 Samuel —
judge and prophet,
voice of the Lord —
died.
All Israel mourned him.

Samuel lived on for many years, saddened at the way things had turned out during Saul's reign. Finally he died. The Book of Samuel says simply, "All Israel assembled and mourned for him, and they buried him in his house at Ramah" (1 Samuel 25:1). Samuel was a bridge between the time of the judges and time of the kings.

Many centuries later, a master of Jewish wisdom, Ben Sirach, sang the praises of Samuel in his book named Sirach after him. (Sometimes it is called Ecclesiasticus, which means "the book of the assembly," or "church.") The Book of Sirach was written about 180 B.C. in order to defend the purity of the Hebrew tradition against the Greek ideas and customs that by then were influencing the Jews. (Roman Catholic Christians include the Book of Sirach in the Bible; most Protestant Christians do not admit it as an official part of the Bible but do read and study it.)

Sirach celebrates the beauty of "wisdom," that is, knowledge tempered with a healthy "fear of the Lord." The book touches upon a wide variety of subjects: the glory of God and the splendor of creation, friendship, the duty of parents, and virtues and vices. The Book of Sirach also has a section which reviews many

great persons in the history of Israel. It presents Samuel as a man of God, a judge, and a prophet.

Samuel, beloved by his Lord,
   a prophet of the Lord, established
     the kingdom
   and anointed rulers over his people.
By the law of the Lord he judged
     the congregation,
   and the Lord watched over Jacob.
By his faithfulness he was proved
     to be a prophet,
   and by his words he became known
     as a trustworthy seer.
He called upon the Lord, the Mighty One,
   when his enemies pressed him on
     every side,
   and he offered in sacrifice a sucking
     lamb.

Then the Lord thundered from heaven,
   and made his voice heard with a
     mighty sound;
   and he wiped out the leaders of the
     people of Tyre
   and all the rulers of the Philistines.
Before the time of his eternal sleep,
   Samuel called men to witness before
     the Lord and his anointed:
"I have not taken any one's property,
   not so much as a pair of shoes."
   And no man accused him.
Even after he had fallen asleep
     he prophesied
   and revealed to the king his death,
   and lifted up his voice out of the earth
     in prophecy,
   to blot out the wickedness of the people.
                (Sirach 46:13-20)

43

One night David had a chance
to kill King Saul.
But David refused to kill
the king chosen by God.
For a time David and Saul
stopped fighting.

David, condemned to be always on the move,
had around six hundred men in his band. In
order to survive, he and his men worked for
Nabal, a rich man with extensive flocks and
herds at Carmel, south of Hebron. It was the
custom to feast after the shearing season. David
sent messengers to ask that his men be allowed
to participate in the feasting. But Nabal rudely
and harshly refused them permission. Angered,
David prepared to take revenge by organizing a
raid on Nabal's household.

Nabal's wife Abigail heard about her husband's rudeness. She decided to try to save the
day. She loaded up some donkeys with good
things to eat and went out to meet David and
his men. She begged David's pardon for her
husband's actions. Nabal, meanwhile, unaware
of what his wife was doing to save his household, carried on with his revelry. In fact, he

drank too much, was stricken with some kind of attack, and died shortly after.

David was impressed with Abigail's act, and he was thankful that he had not killed for revenge. He wooed and married Abigail; he had already married a woman named Ahinoam from Jezreel. (More than one wife was permitted according to the customs of the times.) As for Michal, Saul had given her to someone else when David left.

David's marriage to Abigail, however, changed nothing about his standing as a fugitive. Saul learned that David was living in the wilderness of Ziph. He pursued David there with some three thousand of his best men. Just as he had done with Goliath, David devised a way to win out over Saul's superior forces. He did it by refusing to remain on the defensive and run. Instead, he took a few men and managed during the night to sneak into the center of the camp where Saul and all his men were sleeping. Saul lay there with his spear stuck in the ground next to him. The chief of Saul's guard, Abner, was also asleep; he had not posted any guards.

David's lieutenant, Abishai, was tempted to attack the sleeping men and kill the king. David, however, thought it would be shameful to kill an unarmed, defenseless man, particularly when that man was the king, the anointed of the Lord. So he took Saul's spear and water jar far from his side, and then he and Abishai backed off a ways. When out of range of capture, David called out in a voice loud enough to wake the camp.

"You failed in your duty, Abner! I swear by the living Lord that all of you deserve to die, because you have not protected your master, whom the Lord made king. Look! Where is the king's spear? Where is the water jar that was right by his head?"

Saul recognized David's voice and asked, "David, is that you, my son?"

"Yes, Your Majesty," David answered. And he added, "Why, sir, are you still pursuing me, your servant? What have I done? What crime have I committed?"

Saul answered, "I have done wrong. Come back, David, my son! I will never harm you again, because you have spared my life tonight. I have been a fool! I have done a terrible thing!"

David replied, "Here is your spear, Your Majesty. Let one of your men come over and get it." (1 Samuel 26:16-18, 21-22 TEV)

So Saul was spared, due to David's generous spirit. Several other times, David had opportunities to kill Saul, but he did not ever harm him.

44 Again pursued by Saul, David
and an outlaw band lived
among the Philistines
and became popular there.
Once David rescued the people
of the town of Ziklag,
who had been captured
by the Amalekites.

Saul's good will was short-lived. He again tried
to get rid of David, who he thought wanted to
be king. David decided he had to leave his
country to live in Philistine territory; only then
would he be safe from Saul. So David and his
band of six hundred men went into the service
of a minor Philistine king from Gath named
Achish.

From Ziklag, a town at the edge of Judah, in
the Negeb desert region, David conducted raids
against the neighboring seminomadic peoples,
who were enemies of Judah. He would distri-
bute among the other people of the Negeb the
goods he won in battle. In this way, David
became popular in that area of Judah.

Achish knew nothing of this; he was too busy
preparing to join the other Philistines in an all-
out attack against Israel in the Valley of Jezreel.
Although Achish had expected David to take
part in this battle, some other Philistine leaders

insisted that David could not be trusted in a battle against his fellow Israelites, so he was sent away.

Two days later David and his men arrived back at Ziklag. The Amalekites had raided southern Judah and attacked Ziklag. They had burned down the town and captured all the women; they had not killed anyone, but had taken everyone with them when they left. When David and his men arrived, they found that the town had been burned down and that their wives, sons, and daughters had been carried away. David and his men started crying and did not stop until they were completely exhausted. Even David's two wives, Ahinoam and Abigail, had been taken away.

(1 Samuel 30:1-5 TEV)

David finally stopped weeping, and after offering prayers to the Lord, he began to pursue the Amalekites. Two hundred of David's men were too exhausted to keep up and had to fall behind. David and the others caught up with the marauding band of Amalekites.

And David smote them from twilight until the evening of the next day; and not a man of them escaped, except four hundred young men, who mounted camels and fled. David recovered all that the Amalekites had taken; and David rescued his two wives. Nothing was missing, whether small or great, sons or daughters, spoil or anything that had been taken; David brought back all.

(1 Samuel 30:17-19)

David shared with the elders of Judah much of the victory spoils recovered from the Amalekites.

45 Saul was afraid before a battle
with the Philistines.
So he consulted a sorceress
to talk with the dead Samuel.
Samuel predicted Saul's defeat.
The prediction came true.
Rather than let his enemies
kill him, Saul killed himself.

The Philistine armies were gathered on the
plain of Jezreel, ready to attack the Israelites.
Saul and his troops had rushed to Mount
Gilboa, on the edge of the plain. Saul was no
longer a young warrior, confident that the Lord
was with him. He was worn out with continual
wars; he was weakened by his own jealousy and
by his fears about David. He was so fearful that
he consulted a witch at Endor. The Bible says
that Saul went to see this sorceress in order to
find out in advance the fate that was in store for
him. She supposedly was able to predict the
future by consulting the spirits of the dead.

But since Saul himself had forbidden the
practice of such sorcery, or spiritualism, in
Israel, he had to disguise himself in order to go
to a sorceress himself. It would not do for the
king to be recognized.

Then the woman said, "Whom shall I bring
up for you?" He said, "Bring up Samuel for
me." When the woman saw Samuel, she cried
out with a loud voice; and the woman said to
Saul, "Why have you deceived me? You are
Saul." The king said to her, "Have no fear;

what do you see?" And the woman said to Saul, "I see a god coming up out of the earth." He said to her, "What is his appearance?" And she said, "An old man is coming up; and he is wrapped in a robe." And Saul knew that it was Samuel, and he bowed with his face to the ground, and did obeisance. (1 Samuel 28:11-14)

At this point in the story, the biblical authors report a strange conversation between Saul and the spirit of the dead Samuel. From beyond the grave, Samuel predicted Israel's defeat at the hands of the Philistines and also Saul's own death. Not long after, the prediction was fulfilled.

The Philistines fought a battle against the Israelites on Mount Gilboa. Many Israelites were killed there, and the rest of them, including King Saul and his sons, fled. But the Philistines caught up with them and killed three of Saul's sons, Jonathan, Abinadab, and Malchishua. The fighting was heavy around Saul, and he himself was hit by enemy arrows and badly wounded. He said to the young man carrying his weapons, "Draw your sword and kill me, so that these godless Philistines won't gloat over me and kill me." But the young man was too terrified to do it. So Saul took his own sword and threw himself on it. The young man saw that Saul was dead, so he too threw himself on his own sword and died with Saul. And that is how Saul, his three sons, and the young man died; all of Saul's men died that day. (1 Samuel 31:1-6 TEV)

The Philistines cut off the head of King Saul, stripped off his armor, and nailed his body, along with those of his three sons, to the walls of Beth Shan, a nearby village.

Like most leaders, Saul had his share of success and failure. By comparison with David, who is obviously favored by the biblical writers, Saul's failures appear to outweigh his successes. However, Saul did accomplish a great deal as a skillful military leader who united the Israelites in battle and prevented the Philistines from conquering Canaan. He prepared the way for David to reign over a unified country.

46 Saul's son Jonathan,
the close friend of David,
died in the same battle
as his father.
David mourned over
the deaths of Saul
and Jonathan.

When David learned of the death of Saul and
Jonathan, he mourned according to the custom
of Israel.

> David tore his clothes in sorrow, and all his
> men did the same. They grieved and
> mourned and fasted until evening for Saul
> and Jonathan and for Israel, the people of
> the Lord, because so many had been killed in
> battle. (2 Samuel 1:11-12 TEV)

Many times David had comforted and
soothed Saul by singing to the accompaniment
of his lyre. Now he was inspired to express his
sorrow. He sang a beautiful and dignified song
for those fallen in battle, heroes forever after.
Even though David had been threatened con-
stantly by Saul, he sincerely mourned the death
of Saul, who was the Lord's anointed monarch,
chosen by God to lead the people.

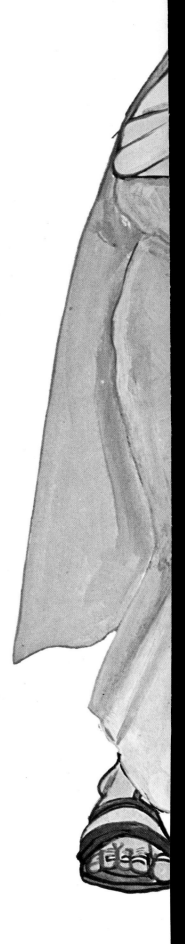

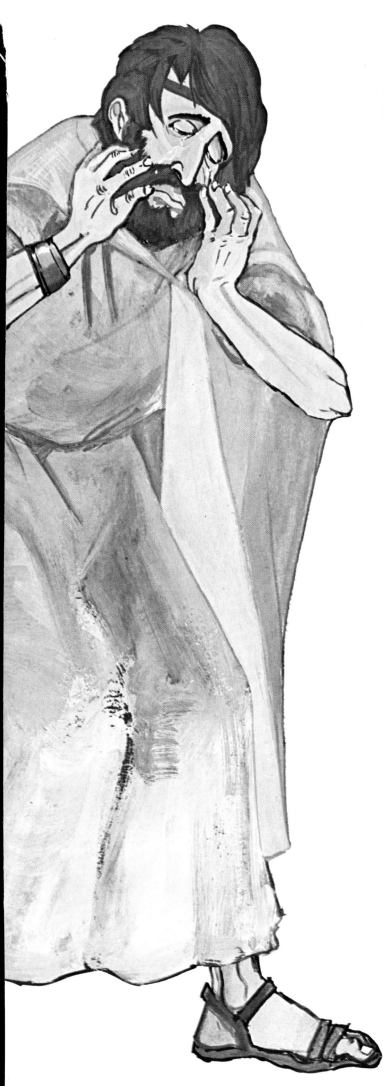

But it was especially in mourning for his friend Jonathan that David found just the right words to express his feelings. This is David's lament for Saul and Jonathan:

"On the hills of Israel our
        leaders are dead!
    The bravest of our soldiers
        have fallen!
Do not announce it in Gath
        or in the streets of Ashkelon.
Do not make the women of
        Philistia glad;
    do not let the daughters of
        pagans rejoice.

Saul and Jonathan, so
        wonderful and dear;
    together in life, together in
        death;
    swifter than eagles, stronger
        than lions.

Women of Israel, mourn for Saul!
    He clothed you in rich
        scarlet dresses
    and adorned you with jewels
        and gold.

The brave soldiers have fallen,
    they were killed in battle.
    Jonathan lies dead in the hills.

I grieve for you, my brother Jonathan;
    how dear you were to me!
How wonderful was your love for me,
    better even than the love of women.

The brave soldiers have fallen,
    their weapons abandoned
        and useless."
            (2 Samuel 1:19-20; 23-27 TEV)

47 After Saul's death the northern tribes challenged David's leadership. David's forces won in battle, and he was accepted as king of all the Israelites.

by the head and plunged his sword into his opponent's side, so that all twenty-four of them fell down dead together. And so that place in Gibeon is called "Field of Swords."

Then a furious battle broke out, and Abner and the Israelites were defeated by David's men. (2 Samuel 2:14-17 TEV)

In the course of the war that followed, two traitors in Ishbosheth's camp assassinated him.

At the time of Saul's death, the twelve Israelite tribes were fighting among themselves. Rivalries were especially strong between the northern and southern areas. In the north were grouped ten of the tribes, whose territory extended all the way to the "country of Aram" (which is modern-day Syria). The south included the territory of the tribe of Simeon, which extended southwards to the Negeb desert and the country of Edom, and the territory of the tribe of Judah, which was the largest and most powerful of all the tribes. And so there were ten tribes on one side and only two on the other.

Those tribes that were loyal to Saul, the northern tribes, did not want to recognize David as king. They placed on the throne one of Saul's sons, a weakling whose name was Ishbosheth. He was afraid of the men of Judah, and moved into the back country of Manhanaim, near the Ammonites.

David seemed much more confident of his mission. Confirmed as king by the men of Judah, he was anointed as king at their hands and reigned from Hebron, the chief city in Judah.

Two kings reigning in the same country could not last long. The first clash broke out in Gibeon, in the territory of Benjamin. Abner, Saul's commander who now supported Ishbosheth, organized with David's general Joab an armed contest between a dozen young men from each camp. This match ended in bloodshed:

> Abner said to Joab, "Let's have some of the young men from each side fight an armed contest."
> "All right," Joab answered.
> So twelve men, representing Ishbosheth and the tribe of Benjamin, fought twelve of David's men. Each man caught his opponent

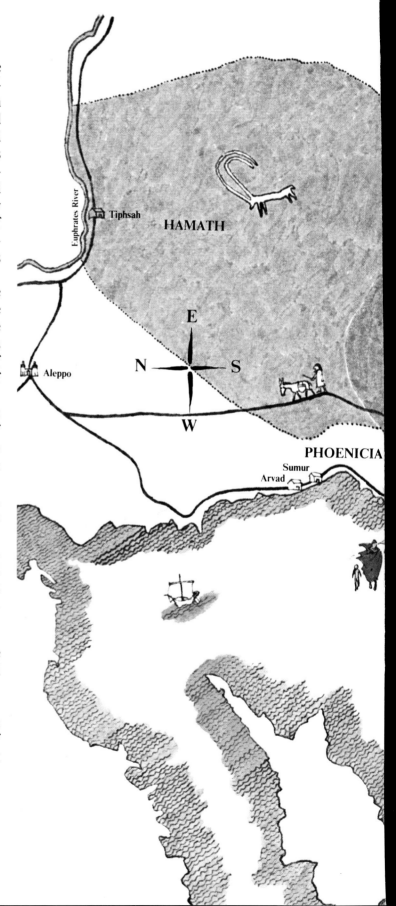

These traitors were hurrying to put themselves on the side of the stronger king.

David could not bear the idea of so terrible a crime against the king, and so he had these two traitors executed. And to demonstrate that he had no ill feeling toward the people in the north, he also adopted the crippled son of his dead friend Jonathan.

The northern tribes no longer had a king, so they decided to recognize the kingship of David.

So all the leaders of Israel came to King David at Hebron. He made a sacred alliance with them, they anointed him, and he became king of Israel. David was thirty years old when he became king, and he ruled for forty years. He ruled in Hebron over Judah for seven and a half years, and in Jerusalem over all Israel and Judah for thirty-three years. (2 Samuel 5:3-5) TEV)

48 Sneaking in through a tunnel,
David's men captured
the fortress of Jerusalem
from the Jebusites.
King David made the city
his new capital.

I was glad when they said to me,
   "Let us go to the house of the Lord!"
Our feet have been standing
   within your gates, O Jerusalem!
Jerusalem, built as a city
   which is bound firmly together,
to which the tribes go up,
   the tribes of the Lord,
as was decreed for Israel,
   to give thanks to the name of the Lord.
                    (Psalm 122:1-4)

Israelite pilgrims sang this psalm as they
climbed up the hill to Jerusalem. Much beloved
by the Jewish people, Jerusalem came to symbolize "the city of peace." It also later became a
symbol of the world to come: All nations would
one day be gathered together in an eternity of
happiness in the New Jerusalem.

This city of great promise began way back in
the Bronze Age. Some Semitic nomads called
Canaanites settled on the land that was to
become the Promised Land, and they gave their
name to it: Canaan. Among these Canaanites,
there was a tribe known as the Jebusites. They
settled on one of the hills that would later form
part of Jerusalem and they established there a
town they called Zion.

The city of Jerusalem was built on a high
ridge bordered by deep valleys, the valleys of
Kidron and Hinnom. It was a fortress that was
almost impossible to penetrate and, for a long
time, the Israelites were unable to conquer it.
David especially wanted to conquer this last
Canaanite stronghold in the central part of the
country. Not only would the city be valuable as
a fortress, but it would also link the north and
the south by its location between the two sides.

But how could David manage to take over
this hill city protected by strong city walls? Certainly not by force. It would have to be taken by
thinking up a new plan of attack.

David's men scouted out the area around the
city and discovered a water tunnel that led into
the city. The main spring which provided fresh
drinking water to the inhabitants of the city was
located outside the city walls, in a cave down in
the valley. In peacetime this presented no problem; the inhabitants simply came out of the city

and went to the spring for water, making use of the city gate called "the gate of waters." In wartime, of course, they couldn't do that, so the Jebusites had hollowed out a tunnel through which they could reach the spring without going outside the city walls in the open.

David's general and some of his men in a daring adventure entered the tunnel through the cave and made their way through it to the heart of the city. They attacked the terrified Jebusites and threw open the city gates.

Taken completely by surprise, the Jebusites did not offer any resistance; they surrendered without striking a blow. David took no action against the local population; he did not even require them to leave the city. And so the king famous for his harp and slingshot established himself in the city of peace.

49 David brought to Jerusalem the ark of the covenant, the symbol of God's presence. David danced for joy as the ark came into the city.

Many years had passed since the young Samuel installed the ark of the covenant at Kiriath-jearim after it had been recovered from the Philistines. Now David was king in Jerusalem, and one of his first concerns was to bring the ark of the covenant into the new capital city, because the ark symbolized the presence of God among his people.

David himself led a delegation to bring the ark out of the house of a man named Abinadab. The ark was carried on a new cart, and a procession of joyful people accompanied the ark.

And David and all the house of Israel were making merry before the Lord with all their might, with songs and lyres and harps and tambourines and castanets and cymbals.

And David danced before the Lord with all his might; and David was girded with a linen ephod, a priestly apron. So David and all the house of Israel brought up the ark of the Lord with shouting, and with the sound of the horn.

And they brought in the ark of the Lord, and set it in its place, inside the tent which David had pitched for it; and David offered burnt offerings and peace offerings before the Lord. (2 Samuel 6:5, 14-15, 17)

Feasting followed these offerings to the Lord. Cakes, dates, and raisins were distributed to all the people. Everyone rejoiced—except one person, Michal, the daughter of Saul and again wife of David. She had watched David dancing before the ark of the Lord as it was brought into the city. Wearing only an ephod, David had exposed his nakedness underneath in front of his servants. Michal was horrified by this, considering it something a king should never do. She scolded David sharply. He replied:

"It was before the Lord, who chose me above your father, and above all his house, to appoint me as prince of Israel, the people of the Lord—and I will make merry before the Lord." (2 Samuel 6:21)

For it was indeed before the Lord that David made merry. God was the King of Kings. This is made clear by Psalms 24 and 47, both of which might have been written to celebrate the enthroning of the ark of the covenant.

Fling wide the gates,
    open the ancient doors.
    and the great king will come in.
Who is this great king?
He is the Lord, strong and mighty.
    the Lord, victorious in battle.
                    (Psalm 24:7-8 TEV)

Clap your hands for joy, all peoples!
    Praise God with loud songs!
The Lord the Most High, is to be feared;
    he is a great king, ruling over all the world.
God goes up to his throne.
    There are shouts of joy
        and the blast of trumpets,
    as the Lord goes up.
                    (Psalm 47:1-2, 5 TEV)

50 David wanted to build a temple
for the ark of the covenant.
The prophet Nathan told David
that David's descendants
would rule in Jerusalem
and that his son Solomon
would build a temple.

After David was installed as king in Jerusalem,
he enjoyed an era of peace. It was quite a
change to be able to occupy himself with something besides war.

David was not content with merely having
brought the ark of the covenant into Jerusalem;
he wanted to build a dwelling place worthy of
the ark, for the ark symbolized the presence of
God among his people. David thought it was
not right that he, a simple human being, should
live in a house made of cedar wood, while the
ark of the Lord was kept in a tent.

He told the prophet Nathan, his trusted ad-
viser, about his plans to construct a suitable
dwelling place for the ark. Later, the Lord inspired Nathan with a thought that Nathan then
communicated to David. What was important
in the eyes of God was not that a temple should
be built for him; rather, God wanted to establish a dynasty of kings from the line of David.

As for the temple, it was destined to be built
by David's son, Solomon. David resigned himself to God's will in the matter.

Then King David went into the Tent of the
Lord's presence, sat down and prayed,
"Sovereign Lord, I am not worthy of what
you have already done for me, nor is my
family. Yet now you are doing even more,
Sovereign Lord; you have made promises
about my descendants in the years to come.
And you let a man see this, Sovereign Lord!
How great you are, Sovereign Lord! There is
none like you; we have always known that
you alone are God. And now, Lord God,
fulfill for all time the promise you made
about me and my descendants, and do what
you said you would.

(2 Samuel 7:18-19, 22, 25 TEV)

Psalm 132 sings of the great place of honor that David enjoys in Israel's history forever. It was composed to celebrate the anniversary of David's bringing of the ark to Jerusalem from Kiriath-jearim.

Remember, O Lord, in David's favor,
    all the hardships he endured;
how he swore to the Lord
    and vowed to the Mighty One of Jacob,
"I will not enter my house
    or get into my bed;
I will not give sleep to my eyes
    or slumber to my eyelids,
until I find a place for the Lord,
    a dwelling place for the Mighty One
        of Jacob."

Lo, we heard of it in Ephrathah,
    we found it in the fields of Jaar.
"Let us go to his dwelling place;
    let us worship at his footstool!"

Arise, O Lord, and go to thy resting
    place,
thou and the ark of thy might.
Let thy priests be clothed with
    righteousness,
For thy servant David's sake
    do not turn away the face
      of thy anointed one.

The Lord swore to David a sure oath
    from which he will not turn back:
"One of the sons of your body
    I will set on your throne.
If your sons keep my covenant
    and my testimonies which I shall
      teach them,
their sons also for ever
    shall sit upon your throne."
             (Psalm 132:1-12)

51 The Bible tells about
David's weakness as well as
his courage and generosity.
David loved Bathsheba,
wife of Uriah,
an army officer,
and she became pregnant.
David then ordered Uriah
into battle; as David hoped,
Uriah was killed.

King David many times showed himself to be a man of strength and courage, as well as a man of largeness of heart and of spirit. He was not, however, a man without faults.

The Bible tells how late one afternoon in the spring, David was out getting some fresh air on the roof of his house overlooking Jerusalem. From there he could see down onto the roofs of other houses below. And on one of the roofs he saw a woman bathing. She was Bathsheba, a woman of great beauty. The king desired her greatly. And since he was the king, no one could say no to him.

David sent for Bathsheba. It turned out that she was the wife of one of his army officers who

was at the front, Uriah the Hittite. Bathsheba eventually became pregnant by David. How could David conceal this adultery from Uriah?

David ordered Uriah to Jerusalem from the battlefront in the hope that Uriah, being with his wife himself, later would think that the child was his own. But Uriah would not go home to his wife while his soldiers were still in the field.

So David had to resort to drastic means to rid himself of Uriah. He sent an order that Uriah was to be placed in the forefront of the hardest fighting. That way, there was a good chance that he would be killed in battle. This was, in fact, what finally happened.

Rid of the embarrassment of having Bathsheba's husband around, David then married her. She later gave birth to his child, a boy. But this child did not survive.

The Lord caused the child that Uriah's wife had borne to David to become very sick. David prayed to God that the child would get well. He refused to eat anything, and every night he went into his room and spent the night lying on the floor.

(2 Samuel 12:15-16 TEV)

But David's sorrowful repentence did not help. The child died. David comforted Bathsheba. Later, she bore him another son, whom David named Solomon.

52 The prophet Nathan came
to King David and told a story
about a rich man stealing
the lamb of a poor man.
David was angry
at the rich man.
"You are the man," said Nathan.
David confessed his sins
of adultery and murder and
prayed for God's forgiveness.

David became very angry at the rich man and said, "I swear by the living Lord that the man who did this ought to die! For having done such a cruel thing, he must pay back four times as much as he took."

"You are that man," Nathan said to David.
(2 Samuel 12:1-7)

David's eyes fell. His heart burned. He confessed his great sin to Nathan. "I have sinned against the Lord" he cried.

David's words are the theme of the famous Psalm 51, the psalm of penitence. This psalm is also known as the *Miserere,* from the first word in its Latin version, which means "Have mercy!" Tradition says that this psalm was written by David himself, with the king as the repentent sinner.

After his terrible crime of having arranged Uriah's death in order to take his wife, David was approached by the prophet Nathan, who told him the following story:

"There were two men who lived in the same town; one was rich and the other poor. The rich man had many cattle and sheep, while the poor man had only one lamb, which he had bought. He took care of it, and it grew up in his home with his children. He would feed it some of his own food, let it drink from his cup, and hold it in his lap. The lamb was like a daughter to him. One day a visitor arrived at the rich man's home. The rich man didn't want to kill one of his own animals to fix a meal for him; instead, he took the poor man's lamb and prepared a meal for his guest."

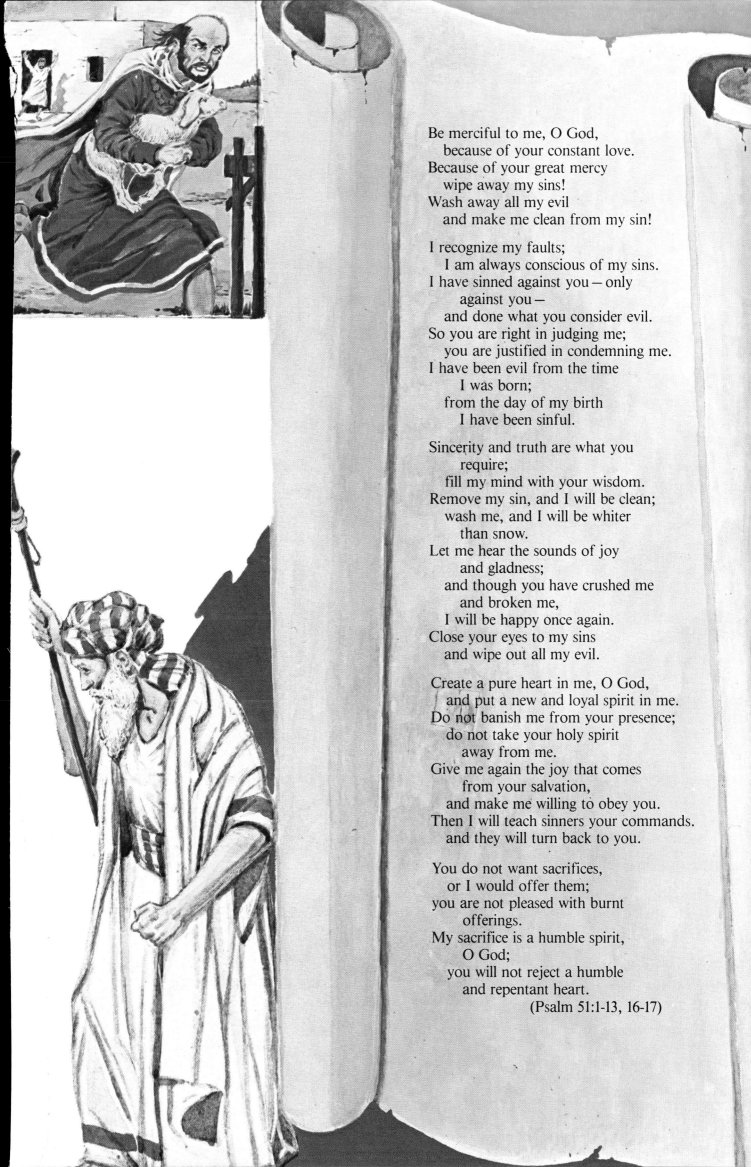

Be merciful to me, O God,
because of your constant love.
Because of your great mercy
wipe away my sins!
Wash away all my evil
and make me clean from my sin!

I recognize my faults;
I am always conscious of my sins.
I have sinned against you — only
against you —
and done what you consider evil.
So you are right in judging me;
you are justified in condemning me.
I have been evil from the time
I was born;
from the day of my birth
I have been sinful.

Sincerity and truth are what you
require;
fill my mind with your wisdom.
Remove my sin, and I will be clean;
wash me, and I will be whiter
than snow.
Let me hear the sounds of joy
and gladness;
and though you have crushed me
and broken me,
I will be happy once again.
Close your eyes to my sins
and wipe out all my evil.

Create a pure heart in me, O God,
and put a new and loyal spirit in me.
Do not banish me from your presence;
do not take your holy spirit
away from me.
Give me again the joy that comes
from your salvation,
and make me willing to obey you.
Then I will teach sinners your commands.
and they will turn back to you.

You do not want sacrifices,
or I would offer them;
you are not pleased with burnt
offerings.
My sacrifice is a humble spirit,
O God;
you will not reject a humble
and repentant heart.
(Psalm 51:1-13, 16-17)

53 One of David's sons, Amnon,
raped his half-sister, Tamar.
In revenge, her brother
Absalom arranged for
the murder of Amnon,
his own half-brother.
Absalom fled for a time
and then later returned
to Jerusalem.
Absalom wanted to overthrow
his father and become king.
He had himself crowned king
at Hebron.
David fled from Jerusalem.

King David's harem of wives and concubines
produced so many children that it was probably
unavoidable that difficulties would arise among
them. And they did. For example, one of
David's older sons, named Amnon, was overcome by the beauty of his half-sister Tamar and
wanted to possess her. This was the source of
great difficulties within David's family.

Tamar was a daughter of David's born to one
of his concubines who was a daughter of
Talmai of Geshur, an Aramean city. The
customs of the time would have allowed
Amnon to ask for the hand in marriage of this
half-sister of his. But instead of doing that,
Amnon raped her. Tamar's full brother Absalom, another of David's sons, was furious.
He arranged to have his half-brother Amnon
killed in order to get revenge for his sister's having been violated. After accomplishing this
deed, Absalom fled to his maternal grand-
father, Talmai, at Geshur, in order to escape
from justice. David was terribly saddened and
upset by this murder between brothers.

Three years passed. By then David had
decided to pardon Absalom, who was back in
Jerusalem. But instead of being grateful for
such a forgiving father, Absalom began to plot
against him. Perhaps he was dreaming of
power himself. Once back in Jerusalem,
Absalom pretended to be friends with
everybody. He set himself up as a judge, and
handled a number of disputes, quarrels, and
other cases. He then used the authority he had
acquired in this way to set people against David
and to make them believe that justice was not
being properly carried out in the kingdom.

Absalom's plot against David finally reached
the point where he was able to take power at
Hebron. In order to gain control in Jerusalem
itself, he needed to get the tribes of Israel in the
north to rebel against David. (There was still

tension between the northern tribes and Judah in the south.) From Hebron,

...he sent messengers to all the tribes of Israel to say, "When you hear the sound of trumpets, shout, 'Absalom has become king at Hebron!'"

"Yes, Your Majesty," they answered. "We are ready to do whatever you say."

(2 Samuel 15:10, 15 TEV)

When David heard this news, he could do nothing but flee, just as he had in Saul's time. Climbing up the Mount of Olives on the other side of the Valley of Kidron, facing Jerusalem, he abandoned the city, leaving behind the ark of the covenant and ten of his concubines. He was accompanied by a few of his valiant men as he left his capital city weeping and in disguise. David not only had to leave his city, but he had to endure the humiliation of insults as well.

Shimei, a man who had been one of Saul's followers, stoned David as he passed by Bahurim. Things had surely reached a low point when "the messiah of the Lord" was treated like this. One of David's faithful followers, Joab, could not stand the insults heaped on his master; he called Shimei a "low dog." But David himself kept silent. He sought only a place to rest and recover from this turn of events. As for Absalom, he installed himself in Jerusalem, where he had himself acclaimed with cries of "Long live the King!"

54 David's army defeated
Absalom's army in battle.
Absalom, caught in an oak tree,
was killed by David's men.
Despite his son's rebellion,
David wept bitterly
at the news of Absalom's death.

Still fleeing, David and his faithful followers crossed the Jordan River near Jericho and headed toward Mahanaim. Absalom and his men pursued them there. It was a strange little war that saw father pitted against son. It was especially strange because the father felt so tenderhearted towards his son and felt no hatred for him at all, but only fear for his safety. David gave strict orders to Joab, the general

leading his army, that he was to treat Absalom leniently:

"Deal gently for my sake with the young man Absalom." And all the people heard the king give orders to the commanders about Absalom.

So the army went out into the field against Israel; and the battle was fought in the forest of Ephraim. (2 Samuel 18:5-6)

Absalom and his men were soundly beaten in battle in Ephraim's forest. David remained safe at Mahanaim; his men had insisted on his staying there in order to insure his safety.

And Absalom chanced to meet the servants of David. Absalom was riding upon his mule, and the mule went under the thick branches of a great oak, and his head caught fast in the oak, and he was left hanging between heaven and earth, while the mule that was under him went on. Joab said, "I will not waste time like this with you." And he took three darts in his hand, and thrust them into the heart of Absalom, while he was still alive in the oak. And ten young men, Joab's armor-bearers, surrounded Absalom and struck him, and killed him.

(2 Samuel 18:9, 14-15)

Several messengers were sent to inform David of the battle's outcome. One of them, a Sudanese slave, arrived, saying,

"I have good news for Your Majesty! Today the Lord has given you victory over all who rebelled against you!"

"Is the young man Absalom all right?" the king asked.

The slave answered, "I wish that what has happened to him would happen to all your enemies, sir, and to all who rebel against you."

The king was overcome with grief. He went up to the room over the gateway and wept. As he went, he cried, "O my son! My son Absalom! Absalom, my son! If only I had died in your place, my son! Absalom, my son!" (2 Samuel 18:31-33 TEV)

David's victory was a terrible victory for him, since his own son's death was one of its results. Nevertheless, David had to overcome his grief so that he didn't give the impression that he was rejecting his own army; he went to the city gates of Mahanaim and met with his loyal men there.

Then David went back to Jerusalem. His return was marked by great mercy; in fact, he pardoned all who had abandoned him and risen up against him, even Shimei who had stoned him.

Following the defeat of Absalom, the people of the northern tribes came back to David. But when David set himself up again in his capital city of Jerusalem, the rivalry between the north and south was stirred up. The people of Israel in the north, jealous of the people of Judah, accused the Judeans of trying unfairly to keep the king to themselves.

55 People in David's time thought that famines and plagues were the punishment of God for some wrongdoing and that they needed to do something to make up for their evil.

During the reign of David his people suffered both famines and plagues. The way the Bible interprets these scourges seems strange to our twentieth-century way of thinking. Here is a story of a famine:

> During David's reign there was a severe famine which lasted for three full years. So David consulted the Lord about it, and the Lord said, "Saul and his family are guilty of murder; he put the people of Gibeon to death." (2 Samuel 21:1)

In ancient Israel, it was generally believed that natural scourges like this were punishments coming from God. And so this famine was attributed to Saul's unfaithfulness in breaking an agreement which had been made with the inhabitants of Gibeon in the time of Joshua; Saul had wrongfully killed a certain number of Gibeonites in the course of his wars. In order to ward off the punishment of famine, the Israelites believed they had to do something to make up for that earlier wrongdoing on Saul's part. So David handed over to the Gibeonites seven descendants of Saul, whom the Gibeonites then hanged on a mountain.

Here is an example of a plague which the people interpreted as coming from an angry God:

> On another occasion the Lord was angry with Israel, and he made David bring trouble on them. The Lord said to him, "Go and count the people of Israel and Judah." So David gave orders to Joab, the commander

of his army; "Go with your officers through all the tribes of Israel from one end of the country to the other, and count the people. I want to know how many there are."

They reported to the king the total number of men capable of military service: 800,000 in Israel and 500,000 in Judah.

But after David had taken the census, his conscience began to hurt, and he said to the Lord, "I have committed a terrible sin in doing this! Please forgive me. I have acted foolishly."

So the Lord sent an epidemic on Israel, which lasted from that morning until the

time that he had chosen. From one end of the country to the other seventy thousand Israelites died.

(2 Samuel 24:1-2, 9, 10, 15 TEV)

Several strands of stories are combined and mixed up in these texts found at the end of the Second Book of Samuel. For that reason, it is difficult to interpret some of the passages found in this part of the Bible, including this case of the "census" of the people of Israel.

To our way of thinking it is illogical for God to urge David to conduct a census and then to punish him for carrying it out. But for the writer of this story, God caused everything both good and bad. (A later writer, in the First Book of Chronicles, changed the interpretation of this story by saying that "Satan" caused David to conduct the census.) The taking of the census upset the people because they knew it was to get more taxes and to conscript people for the king's army.

To ward off the plague, David wanted to do something to make up for his census taking. So he purchased a special piece of land in Jerusalem where animals had been stabled.

Then he built an altar to the Lord and offered burnt offerings and fellowship offerings. The Lord answered his prayer, and the epidemic in Israel was stopped.

(2 Samuel 24:25 TEV)

Many believe that on this very piece of land, which was purchased from a Jebusite named Araunah, the Temple of Solomon was later built.

56 David became a famous king, and Israel was at peace. David expressed his love for God in the poetry of his psalms.

Following the revolt of Absalom, David had yet another revolt, the rebellion of a man named Sheba, to contend with. He appointed Amasa to quell this rebellion, but when Amasa was slow in carrying out the king's orders, David sent Joab and other soldiers after Sheba.

Sheba sought refuge at Abel of Beth-Maach, in the northernmost part of Israel. But he was unable to escape for long. A woman of the town betrayed him, persuaded the people to cut off his head, and then threw it over the wall to Joab.

Little by little over the years, David acquired great standing in the eyes of the neighboring peoples. He finally defeated the Philistines and made them his vassals (people subject to him). Other neighboring peoples — the Ammonites, the Edomites, and the Moabites — also paid tribute to him. The court of the Jewish king became famous.

David's immediate group of followers was made up of his "valiant men," faithful companions who had followed him from his earliest days as a leader and had suffered with him through all his struggles when he was being pursued by Saul. The king also enjoyed the services of a scribe, a record keeper, and a number of counselors. A personal bodyguard was responsible for his safety.

David ruled the heads of the twelve tribes and also settled the disputes that arose among his people. He appointed a superintendent of public works, who drafted citizens to work for the benefit of the country without pay. Royal administrators looked after the property of the king: vineyards, olive groves, and flocks and herds.

The army, a key institution in the kingdom, was headed by Joab, a violent man but an excellent soldier.

Religion naturally played a very important role at the court of King David. The ark of the covenant was kept within the confines of the royal palace. There was an organized clergy that was divided into twenty-four classes of priests.

Even after he became king, David still remained the poet he had always been. He personally supervised the musicians at the religious services and also the chanting of the psalms, some of which he wrote himself.

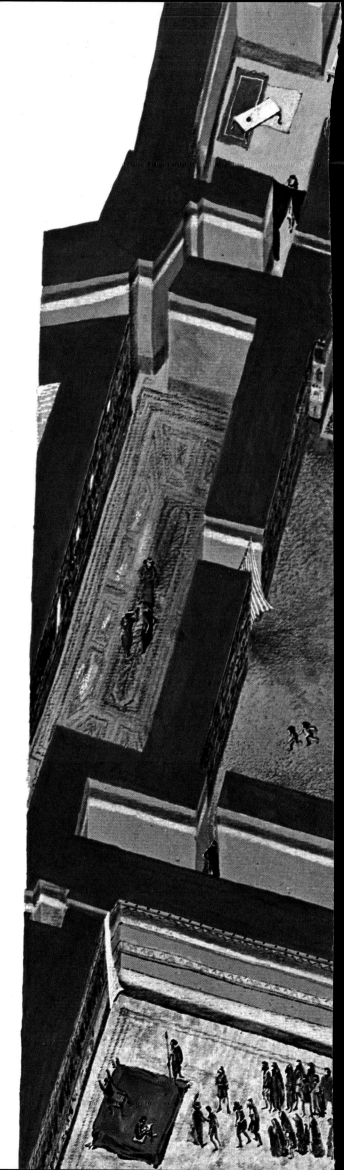

Then King David sent for Zadok, Nathan, and Benaiah. When they came in, he said to them, "Take my court officials with you; have my son Solomon ride my own mule, and escort him down to Gihon Spring, where Zadok and Nathan are to anoint him as king of Israel. Then blow the trumpet and shout, 'Long live King Solomon!' Follow him back here when he comes to sit on my throne. He will succeed me as king, because he is the one I have chosen to be the ruler of Israel and Judah." (2 Kings 1:32-35 TEV)

57 When David was very old, fights began over his throne. David made sure that his son Solomon was proclaimed King. Then David, who had received a wonderful promise from the Lord, died.

Now King David was old and advanced in years; and although they covered him with clothes, he could not get warm. Therefore his servants said to him, "Let a young maiden be sought for my lord the king, and let her wait upon the king, and be his nurse; let her lie in your bosom, that my lord the king may be warm." (1 Kings 1:1-2)

When the death of David was close, rivalries and plots to gain the throne became intense. One of David's sons, Adonijah, for example, spread the word everywhere that he was going to be the new king. He was a half-brother of Absalom and of Solomon, the son of Bathsheba. His age and rank both made him think perhaps he would inherit the throne. And he began to act as if he had already inherited it. He offered the customary sacrifice at Enrogel, in the presence of the army chiefs and of the priest Abiathar; and then he proclaimed himself king.

But Bathsheba wasn't willing to accept this. Supported by the prophet Nathan as well as by the priest Zadok, she went before David to inform him of Adonijah's takeover of power and to remind him of his promises to her about her son Solomon. She reminded David that he had said to her, "Solomon, your son, shall reign after me, and he shall sit upon my throne." David was faithful to his word.

When David was about to die, he called his son Solomon and gave him his last instructions: "My time to die has come. Be confident and determined, and do what the Lord your God orders you to do. Obey all his laws and commands, as written in the Law of Moses, so that wherever you go you may prosper in everything you do. If you obey him, the Lord will keep the promise he made when he told me that my descendants would rule Israel as long as they were careful to obey his commands faithfully with all their heart and soul.   (1 Kings 2:1-4 TEV)

The Bible says that David then spoke his last words, words which sound much like the poetry of the psalms.

The spirit of the Lord speaks through me;
    his message is on my lips.
The God of Israel has spoken;
    the protector of Israel said to me:
"The King who rules with justice,
    who rules in reverence for God,
is like the sun shining on a cloudless dawn,
    the sun that makes the grass
        sparkle after rain."
And that is how God will bless
    my descendants,
    because he has made an
        eternal covenant with me,
    an agreement that will not be broken,
    a promise that will not be changed.
                (2 Samuel 23:2-5 TEV)

Then David joined his ancestors in death and was buried.

58 Here are some key words
and ideas found
in the Bible stories
which tell about
the period of time
from Joshua until David:

the twelve tribes of Israel
the period of the judges
the monarchy
Jerusalem
the dynasty of David

The Twelve Tribes of Israel

Twelve. There are twelve months in the year, twelve signs of the zodiac. The number twelve appears in the writings of many people; usually it suggests unity, or wholeness.

In the Bible the number twelve means a fullness, a completion, or a perfection. There are twelve tribes of Israel — descended from the twelve sons of Jacob. In the Gospel we read how Jesus chose twelve apostles and seventy-two disciples. The Book of Revelation in the Bible often uses the number twelve to symbolize the accomplishment of all things: The gates of the heavenly city of Jerusalem are twelve in number, as are the foundations. And among the elect, twelve thousand from each of the twelve tribes of Israel have their foreheads marked with a particular sign.

The Period of the Judges

For about two hundred years — from the death of Joshua until the establishment of the monarchy — the Israelite people were led by judges. These men and women did not rule over all of the tribes. They ruled periodically over specific tribes as the need arose to defend Israel against her enemies. Believed to be especially gifted with the courage and wisdom, the judges were military leaders, spiritual leaders (of varying degrees of holiness), and persons who settled disputes.

The stories of the twelve judges are told in the Book of Judges, which was not written until later, during the monarchy. The writers viewed the people as backtracking on their commitment to the Lord; the stories have a common theme: sin, punishment, repentance, and forgiveness. Whenever the people rebelled against the Lord, pagan nations defeated them; whenever they repented, the Lord sent judges to save them.

Besides the twelve judges presented in the Book of Judges, two other judges — Eli and Samuel — are presented in First Samuel. Samuel is considered to be the last judge and the first prophet.

The Monarchy

The Book of Judges describes Israelite life during the period of the judges: "In those days there was no king in Israel; every man did what was right in his own eyes." Added to the lack of order during this time was the problem of constant trouble with the enemies of Israel, particularly the Philistines. The people began to demand a king, to unify the tribes into a nation

and strengthen them against outsiders. They wanted a king like the other nations had.

Samuel realized the dangers of a human kingship: loss of freedom, heavy taxes, forced labor, and military service. But finally, when it seemed to be the Lord's will, Samuel agreed to select a king for the people.

Saul was the first king. He achieved some military success against the Philistines, but David was the military genius who completely subdued them. He created a standing army and set up many different court officials. David took advantage of a time during which the traditionally powerful nations in the area were busy elsewhere to expand greatly his kingdom, later inherited by his son Solomon.

Jerusalem

David captured the hill city of Jerusalem from the Jebusites and made it Israel's center of government and worship. The city was a good choice because it was located on neutral territory between the northern tribes, who called their land Israel, and the southern tribes, located in David's Judah.

Jerusalem has become a symbol of future happiness and peace. The author of the Book of Revelation in the New Testament shared this splendid vision with us: "I saw the holy city, the New Jerusalem, coming down out of heaven from God, prepared as a bride adorned for her husband" (Revelation 21:2).

The Dynasty of David

The Lord promised David, through the prophet Nathan, that an uninterrupted line of his descendants would follow him on the throne in Jerusalem. When the kingdom of Judah was defeated in 587 B.C., and many people deported to Babylon, was this the end of the dynasty of David? It did not turn out that way. The promise of the Lord did not refer merely to an earthly kingdom — it referred to the Kingdom of God. From the dynasty of David was to come the true Messiah, who proclaimed that the Kingdom of God is at hand. The prophet Isaiah told King Ahaz in a famous prophecy: "Therefore the Lord himself will give you a sign: Behold, a young woman shall conceive and bear a son, and shall call his name Immanuel" (Isaiah 7:14).

The first Christians believed that Jesus the Christ fulfilled this prophecy. For them Jesus was Immanuel, which means "God is with us." Jesus thus brings the dynasty of David to completion.

59 Here are some more important words and ideas found in the Bible stories from Joshua to David:

holy war
the Messiah
the ark of the covenant
Nathan's prophecy

Holy War

From the time they first entered the Promised Land, from the time of the ancient judges until the time of David, the Israelites fought wars with the surrounding peoples who attacked them. For Israel this was a question of life or death. These wars were considered "holy wars," for the biblical writers believed that God was leading the people into possession of the Promised Land. War was an event in which God fought for the people. Whether the result was victory or defeat, they saw God's will expressed in the outcome. It was not surprising that war was viewed as a kind of "religious rite." For the Israelites, war was accompanied by definite ways of behaving. They were forbidden to plunder their enemies; the booty of war belonged to God. The idea of a holy war is very difficult for us to understand.

The Messiah

The word *messiah* comes from the Hebrew word Mashiah, which means "anointed," or "consecrated by anointing with oil." Messiah was the title given to the king when he was anointed by a prophet or other representative of God who poured oil on his head. David became the ideal "messiah" in Israel. From the descendants of David Israel expected the Messiah who would save his people once and for all.

When the Bible was translated from Hebrew into Greek, the Hebrew word *messiah* became the Greek word *Christos,* which also means "anointed." Because the New Testament was written in Greek, Jesus came to be called Jesus the Christ.

Nathan's Prophecy

Nathan, prophet and advisor, spoke the words of the Lord to David: "I will make for you a great name...I will raise up your offspring after you...He shall build a house for my name, and I will establish the throne of his kingdom for ever...And your house and your kingdom shall be made sure for ever before me; your throne shall be established forever."

This prophecy was one of the most important in Israel's history. The Lord's covenant with his people was now attached specifically to the kings in David's line. The people began to focus on a future king who would bring a time of God's rule over all people.

The Ark of the Covenant

The ark of the covenant was a hardwood chest plated with gold, and carried by two gold-covered poles which were run through golden rings attached to its base. It contained two stone tablets, on which were carved the Ten Commandments, and other sacred objects. As the symbol of God's presence among the Israelites, it accompanied them during their wanderings in the desert and during the ups and downs of their conquest of the Promised Land. Sometimes the Israelites carried the ark with them in battle.

When David became king, he brought the ark to Jerusalem to make the city into a holy place and the religious center of all Israel. When David's son Solomon built the Temple, the ark was kept in the innermost sanctuary. No one knows what happened to the ark when the Temple was destroyed in 587 B.C. by the Babylonians.

Outline by Chapter

IN THE PROMISED LAND

CHAPTER